WORLD BANK STUDY

Trade and Transport Facilitation Assessment

A Practical Toolkit for Country Implementation

THE WORLD BANK
Washington, D.C.

Manufactured in the United States of America
First Printing: June 2010

Printed on recycled paper

1 2 3 4 13 12 11 10

World Bank Studies are published to communicate the results of the Bank's work to the development community with the least possible delay. The manuscript of this paper therefore has not been prepared in accordance with the procedures appropriate to formally-edited texts. Some sources cited in this paper may be informal documents that are not readily available.

ISBN-13: 978-0-8213-8412-1
eISBN: 978-0-8213-8413-8
ISSN: 1726-5878 DOI: 10.1596/978-0-8213-8412-1

Library of Congress Cataloging-in-Publication Data has been requested.

Contents

Tables

Figures

Boxes

Foreword

Trade facilitation and logistics have become an important policy area in development. Supply chain constraints are now recognized as a major impediment to export-led growth.

The Trade and Transport Facilitation Assessment is a practical tool to identify the obstacles to the fluidity of trade supply chains. Taking the perspective of service delivery to traders, the TTFA assessment is founded on facts and data collected through a series of meetings and interviews with the main public and private participants to these international supply chains. They include customs and other border agencies, transport regulators, freight forwarders, transport operators, ports, and others. The toolkit helps design plans of action to improve logistics performance among its three main dimensions: infrastructure, services, and procedures and processes.

This new edition of the toolkit provides an opportunity not only to reflect the changes in the trade environment and the need for additional features in the toolkit, but also to benefit from the experiences of the assessments already undertaken based on the original edition. In 2001, the Bank issued a first Trade and Transport Facilitation Audit (TTFA) toolkit based on an original concept developed by John Raven. This initial concept was extensively revised to give the new toolkit an increased operational focus. The semantic change from audit to assessment also reflects the expansion in scope and the emphasis on development of implementable actions beyond the initial diagnosis.

The experience of implementation of the TTFA proved the relevance and the ease of using this instrument. Since 2001, it has benefited many countries, from least-developed countries to emerging economies, as part of the preparation of trade or transport projects, such as corridor development. Trade facilitation is increasingly becoming a key priority to governments at the highest level—as in Indonesia and Morocco, for example—spurred by the realization that logistical bottlenecks were preventing growth opportunities from materializing. They decided to launch ambitious programs starting with an in-depth trade and transport facilitation assessment. This wide body of experience is reflected in this document.

We hope that the toolkit will appeal to a wider audience, including policy makers, economists, development agencies, private sector, and academia. We also hope that it leads to an expansion of the pool of global and local skills available for trade facilitation and logistics activities. The toolkit is designed to help by providing a first cut at identifying the bottlenecks and break the ground for in-depth work. Its scope is very comprehensive, yet it is not an encyclopedia of trade and logistics, but rather a guidebook. Readers in need of more information in any of the specific sub-areas are invited to use specialized resources made available by various international sources. The World Bank is currently issuing toolkits for border management, port reform, supply chain security, and transit corridors.

We are fully confident that this document will be a useful guide that will help implement this important agenda in an increasing number of countries.

Mona Haddad
Sector Manager International Trade
The World Bank

Marc Juhel
Sector Manager Transport
The World Bank

Acknowledgments

This toolkit was prepared by the World Bank's International Trade Department (PRMTR), in close collaboration with the World Bank's Transport Sector unit (ETWTR). Under the supportive guidance of Bernard Hoekman (director) and Mona Haddad (sector manager), this toolkit was prepared by Monica Alina Mustra and Jean-François Arvis[1] and a core team of experts, including John Arnold, Robin Carruthers, and Daniel Saslavsky.

The team is especially indebted to John Raven and Marc Juhel, who had the initial idea of the methodology and prepared the first version of the Toolkit in 2001. Critical inputs were also provided by Brendan Horton, Graham Smith, and Professor Lauri Ojala (Turku School of Economics), who greatly helped improve the concept and content of the Toolkit with their unique experience of actually implementing these assessments in many different regions in the world.

The project greatly benefited from valuable technical expertise and useful comments received from colleagues throughout the drafting process of the report. They included peer reviewers Tomas Serebrisky, Henry Kerali, Michel Bellier, and Philip English, and other colleagues including Abdelmoula Ghzala, Cordula Rastogi, Graham Smith, Charles Kunaka, Gerard McLinden, Jean Christophe Maur, Philip Schuler, Jean-Pierre Chauffour, Krista Lucenti, Patricia Macchi, and Gaël Raballand. Participants in the World Bank's trade facilitation training event on May 4, 2009 also provided constructive feedback.

Moreover, we would like to acknowledge the excellent program support and research assistance provided by Stacey Tai Sie Chow, Kahina Mildrana Robinson, and Anita Nyajur. The report benefited from an editing review by Communications Development Incorporated, Washington, DC. The CD containing the Interview Guide was designed by Anita Nyajur under the close guidance of the core team. Their contributions throughout the publication and dissemination process of this report made this project possible.

Finally, the authors would express their gratitude to the many policy makers and country staff in the World Bank, which supported the implementation of trade and transport facilitation assessments in over 50 countries and helped get the mileage necessary to refine the product and prepare this document.

We hope that this publication will encourage further substantive discussion on this topic.

Note

[1] mmustra@worldbank.org, jarvis1@worldbank.org

Acronyms and Abbreviations

CAD	Cash against documents
CIF	Cost, insurance, freight
FOB	Freight on board *or* free on board
LPI	Logistics Performance Index
TIR	Transports Internationaux Routiers (International Road Transport)
TTFA	Trade and Transport Facilitation Assessment
UNCITRAL	United Nations Commission on International Trade Law
UNCTAD	United Nations Commission on Trade and Development
UNECE	United Nations Economic Commission for Europe
UNESCAP	United Nations Economic and Social Commission for Asia and the Pacific
USITC	United States International Trade Commission
VAT	Value-added tax

CHAPTER 1

What Is the Trade and Transport Facilitation Assessment Toolkit?

Practical trade facilitation reform has become a key development priority in recent years. In 2001, the World Bank issued the first Trade and Transport Facilitation Assessment (TTFA) toolkit.[1] A simple and cost-effective instrument to analyze bottlenecks in international supply chains and prepare corrective measures, the TTFA is designed for any audience interested in trade facilitation and logistics in developing countries, including:

- policy makers in developing countries
- development practitioners, including staff of the World Bank or other development agencies, such as country economists or operational task managers, who are supervising implementation of trade assessments
- trade and transport facilitation consultants or consulting firms.

The TTFA's key insight is that considerable knowledge can easily be obtained by interviewing key participants in the commercial and procedural transactions that form international supply chains, including private service providers such as freight forwarders, exporters, transporters, and bankers, as well as public agencies such as customs, port authorities, and transport regulators.

Why Conduct a TTFA?

A TTFA can inform policy makers on how the supply chains for international trade function and where opportunities exist to improve their performance. Although trade and freight logistics are usually private sector activities, governments play an essential role in improving trade logistics and competitiveness. Regulation of logistics services and trade procedures influences the performance of international supply chains, as does the quality and capacity of public infrastructure. Countries wishing to improve trade logistics may need to reform and modernize border management institutions, change transport regulation policy, and, in some cases, invest significantly in trade-related infrastructure. As the 2007 and 2010 Logistics Performance Index[2] highlighted, a trade supply chain is only as strong as its weakest link. Determining where the weakest links are and addressing them through targeted development interventions has therefore become a major element of the trade facilitation and logistics agenda. A TTFA can help guide these targeted interviews.

Policies that affect trade and logistics regulations and procedures should be built on an understanding of their impact on trade competitiveness. Until recently, policy makers and private sector stakeholders have not had the benchmarking data they needed to identify trade constraints or create constituencies for reform. The Logistics Performance Index (LPI) filled that gap. By providing comprehensive data on country performance and a broad indication of where problems are, the 2007 LPI helped raise awareness and intensified the dialogue between policy makers and the private sector in several countries about logistics bottlenecks and priorities for reform in facilitating international trade and transportation at the country or subregional level.

But making trade logistics work for competitiveness at the country or subregional level requires more than just raising awareness through indicators like the LPI. Understanding the impediments to trade service delivery requires a variety of different analytical approaches and action plans. The TTFA is the primary instrument to respond to this need. It provides an in-depth multidimensional assessment of the performance of services and processes. TTFA can be expanded to include more specific components including:

- supply chain analysis in key sectors (textile, automotive, agriculture, and distribution)
- user surveys
- thematic studies (skills and training, regional logistics, use of information technologies).

Whether narrow or broader, TTFAs require strong client participation from interagency and private–public sector working groups.

What's New in the 2010 Toolkit?

While the first edition of the TTFA concentrated on activities and transactions occurring at the borders and international gateways, this new edition incorporates these border processes into a broader examination of the performance of international supply chains. This second edition of the TTFA toolkit was developed to meet the growing demand for facilitation reforms in an environment of increasing global competition, expanded trade in intermediate goods, and greater synchronicity in the supply of inputs to production and the delivery of products to point of sale. The new, two-phase assessment retains a focus on simplification and harmonization of trade-related procedures but complements this with an examination of the opportunities for improving logistics services, infrastructure, and the overall performance of specific supply chains. This expanded scope reflects the practical evolution of the operational concept of trade facilitation in the context of developing countries.

As in the original toolkit, this new edition uses a basic methodology of interviews with private and public participants in the supply chains. But the interviews are now open-ended, replacing a structured questionnaire with a guide to what topics to include in the interview and how to interpret them. These open-ended interview guides allow the interviewer to construct questions customized for the interviewee's area and level of knowledge and for the structure of the international supply chains in that country.

The new assessment is designed to be implemented in two phases. Both phases involve stakeholders and agencies in the design of the assessment, analysis of findings, and implementation of the projects that may result.

Phase 1 is similar to the original TTFA, intended to provide an understanding of the general problems in infrastructure, regulations, transport and logistics services, and border procedures that affect trade competitiveness in the country or region being assessed. It can be implemented rapidly by a small team. This phase 1dentifies general bottlenecks and provides the focus and organization for phase 2. The expected output of phase 1 includes a preliminary report and concept note for the phase 2 assessment, that incorporates the scope of work for the assessment team and the mode of interaction with the focal point in the country.

The phase 1 assessment alone may be sufficient to develop projects and modernization activities for smaller economies with limited diversity in their supply chains (such as least developed countries). In such cases, a final phase 1 report or policy note can be used to recommend specific project components. A phase 1 report may also be adequate in larger economies, in the context of an update or as a contribution to a broader assessment of competitiveness.

Phase 2 examines the relative importance of the problems identified in the phase 1 assessment, as well as the constraints and needs of specific international supply chains. This phase 1s intended to define a plan of action that includes a series of project components. It permits an in-depth assessment of the relative importance of the problems identified in supply chain performance and of how services within a supply chain add value to traded goods. Phase 2 requires substantial resources mobilized over several months, including a team of experts in different trade and logistics areas.

Guide to the Toolkit

This toolkit provides a conceptual framework and specific schedules and worksheets for planning and conducting a one- or two-phase TTFA. Chapter 2 introduces the supply chain conceptual framework for the TTFA and provides a brief summary of its key activities and decision points. Chapter 3 describes how to implement the assessment, including planning and scheduling, resource requirements, organization of the analysis, and preparation of the reports. Chapter 4 provides case studies from past assessments about two common challenges encountered by trade facilitation assessments: the effects of different levels of government participation in assessments, and common barriers to identifying bottlenecks in supply chains. The appendixes provide additional tools and information on the concept, methodology, and content of the assessment. The accompanying Interview Guide includes a scope for the interviews and checklists for all categories of interviewees and field visits.

Notes

[1] Raven (2001). The first edition of the TTFA toolkit was widely disseminated. It is available online at the Global Facilitation Partnership Web site, http://www.gfptt.org.

[2] Arvis et al. (2007); Arvis et al. (2010). The Logistics Performance Index is a comprehensive benchmarking tool created to help countries identify the challenges and opportunities they face in their performance on trade logistics and what they can do to improve their performance. For more information, please visit www.worldbank.org/lpi.

CHAPTER 2

Conceptual Framework

The Trade and Transport Facilitation Assessment (TTFA) is a tool for identifying inefficiencies in international supply chains that limit a country's ability to compete in international trade. The assessment examines problems that affect not only exports' competitiveness, but also the ability to import and distribute inputs to production and consumer goods.

The assessment acquires this knowledge through a series of structured interviews with key participants in the commercial or procedural transactions that make up an international supply chain. These participants include private service providers, such as freight forwarders, consolidators, transport operators, and financial intermediaries, as well as public agencies, such as customs, other border management agencies, port authorities, and transport regulators. By integrating this knowledge in a supply chain analysis, the assessment helps to identify corrective measures to facilitate trade and transportation and improve competitiveness.

Defining the Objectives of the Assessment

The set of objectives pursued in a TTFA varies to meet each individual country's needs. Because an assessment's scope can become quite broad, it is important to carefully define its objectives, starting with a statement of what the results will be used for. Reasons for undertaking an assessment might include:

- to support a policy dialogue on the opportunities and mechanisms available for improving trade and competitiveness through better freight logistics
- to identify project components that will increase the effectiveness of new infrastructure or guide an effort to strengthen institutions.

Globalized competition and greater supply-chain synchronicity needs have recently spurred demand for deeper facilitation reforms. In this context, a TTFA might pursue two different, specific objectives either jointly or separately. Depending on the needs of each country, the assessment might be oriented to inform country economic policies, or to develop action and reform plans to enhance trade competitiveness.

Figure 2.1. Activities and Outputs Flowchart, Two-phase Trade and Transport Facilitation Assessment

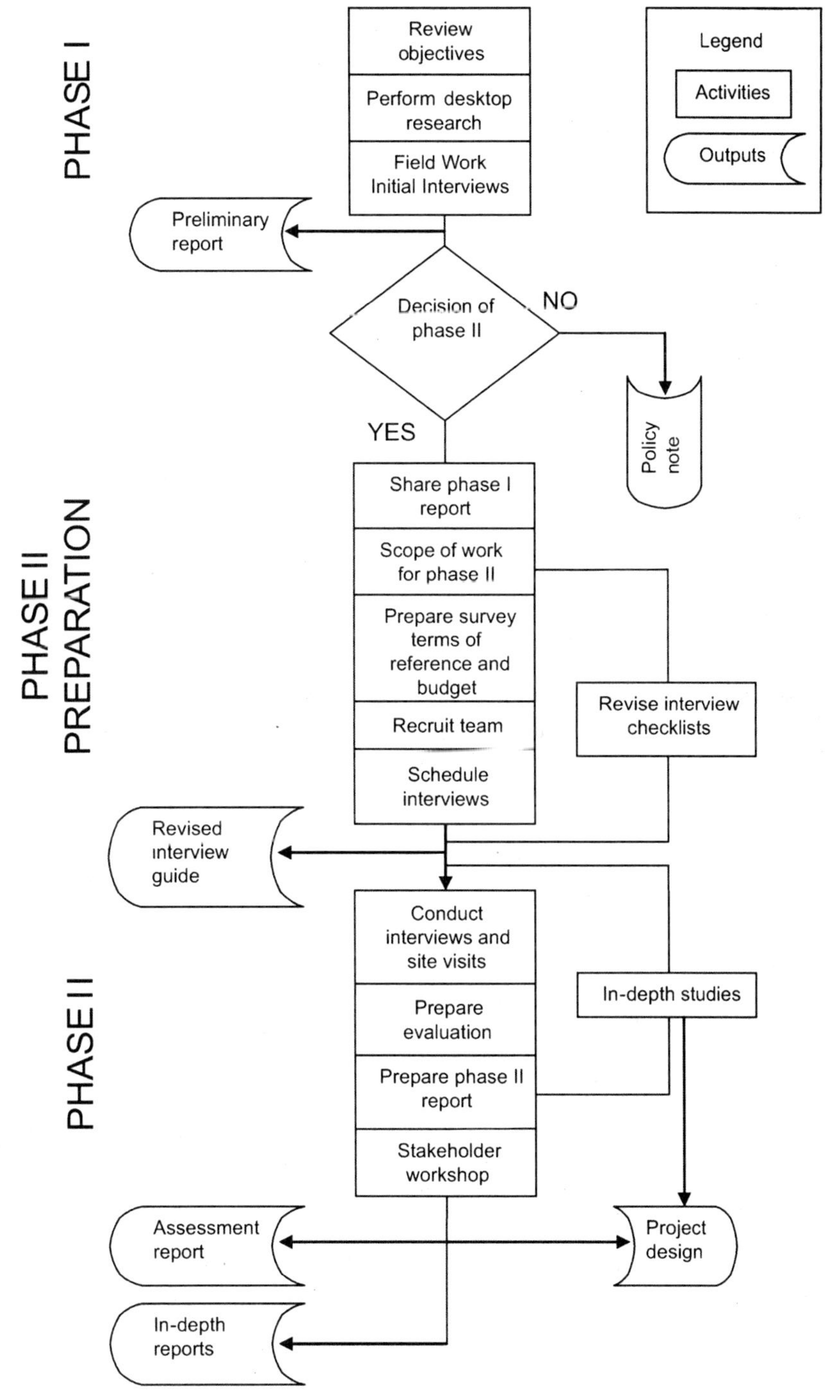

Source: Authors.

Informing Country Economic Policies

The TTFA has become a frequent source of information for other analytical products focused on trade competitiveness, such as the World Bank Group's Diagnostic Trade Integration Studies and Country Economic Memoranda. In this context, the TTFA is a useful instrument to disseminate trade facilitation priorities and key issues to Bank Group staff in charge of operational and economic sector work, such as country economists or task managers.

The TTFA is also intended to serve the policymaking community and development practitioners in general. The assessment might provide information useful to different multilateral institutions, governments, development agencies, and private consultants. For example, a phase 1 assessment might provide background information for scoping work or diagnostic trade competitiveness studies, and preparation material for the inception phase of projects undertaken by consultancy firms. A phase 2 assessment might provide supply chain-specific information, useful for detailed analysis of a particular trade as well as for performance measurement.

Developing Action and Reform Plans to Enhance Trade Competitiveness

The original version of the TTFA primarily collected information on the structure of the logistics sector in various countries. Any resulting trade facilitation projects were usually in customs reform. But a new understanding of how the cost-effective movement of goods is deeply affected by a number of cross-cutting, intertwined policy areas has expanded client needs. The main challenge for the new, two-phase assessment is to provide the tools to translate particular impediments to trade into concrete remedies or action proposals.

For this purpose, the new TTFA toolkit offers a framework to analyze the obstacles affecting a typical supply chain and a list of remedies or action plans, consisting of specific project components.[1] The toolkit also provides a checklist of policy areas and participants needed for the design of different types of project components. These suggested components build on international efforts to introduce best practices and meet performance benchmarks in the following policy areas:[2]

- **Tools and institutions to measure and assess logistics performance**. Develop logistics and facilitation observatories and performance indicators.
- **Institutions and regulations**. Improve international transport agreements, allow foreign participation in logistics services, and reduce economic regulation of transport services.
- **Regulation, quality, and reliability of transport and logistics services and business practices.** Modify policies and regulations that affect the organization of the sector to improve the quality of logistics services. These projects might provide technical assistance to introduce professional standards, certification, and contracts for logistics service providers, and to promote the expansion, integration, and upgrading of scope and scale of services offered.[3] In practice, most advances in freight logistics and supply chain management have involved introducing information and communications technologies to these processes; along with supply management techniques and other mechanisms for self-regulation.

- **Customs modernization**. Reform customs procedures, improve border facilities, and introduce risk management programs to expedite clearance for high compliers. Improve trade security, automatize and simplify other border agencies, and enhance coordination with customs. Introduce single window systems, supported by improvements in information and communication technology.
- **Related procedures and trade facilitation**. Address topics such as simplification of trade and infrastructure tariffs and reduce certification requirements for controlled commodities. Revise domestic tax policy to facilitate movement of goods, and reform banking practices and exchange controls to improve trade. Provide assistance to introduce e-government services, strengthen the capacity of the authorities regulating trade and logistics, and improve the collection, analysis, and monitoring of statistical and performance indicators and policies.
- **Transit regime; air and sea connectivity and liberalization of services**. Plan and manage multimodal freight corridors, and develop urban and line-haul transport interface.
- **Public infrastructure**. Increase private sector participation to provide and maintain public infrastructure, and introduce commercial management to airport and port operations. Also upgrade and construct new transport links, plan and manage multicountry freight corridors, and establish dry ports and inland clearance facilities. Finally, develop logistics hubs and improve telecommunications services to support logistics.

Scope of the Assessment: One or Two Phases?

This new, more comprehensive version of the assessment broadly examines the performance of international supply chains to identify components of the supply chain that introduce avoidable costs, delays, and uncertainty. To accomplish this, the assessment incorporates a broader set of topics in its analysis, including logistics infrastructure, procedures for moving goods, regulatory activities, and the provision, quality, and cost of available logistics services.[4]

Although most assessments will be conducted for single countries, the TTFA's primary focus on international supply chains makes it possible to implement them within other geographical areas, such as international trade corridors (for example, as a regional trade facilitation assessment in West Africa, South Asia, or Central Asia) and regions within large countries (for example, India or Brazil).

The TTFA is conducted in two phases to accommodate different requirements and objectives (see table 2.1). This two-phase procedure allows the assessment to be tailored to the country's specific needs. Though both phases rely on the same conceptual framework, they require different government commitment, resources, duration, scope of work, and final outcome (figure 2.1).

Figure 2.2. Logistics Services in a Typical Supply Chain

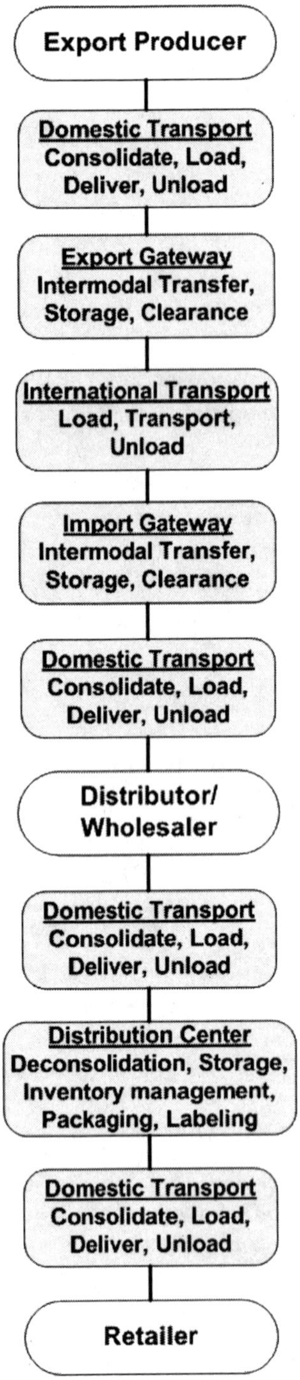

Source: Authors.

Table 2.1. Distinct Characteristics of Assessment Phases I and II

	Phase 1 assessment	Phase 2 assessment
Government commitment	Approval, participation of government officials in discussion with agencies supporting and regulating trade and logistics	Active participation, steering committee
Resources (consultant)	One international logistics expert, plus local consultant	Multidisciplinary team
Duration	3–8 weeks for main expert, one field trip	6–12 months, several field trips
Scope of work	Generic scope based on interviews and visit	Generic scope of work complemented by targeted components (supply chains for specific products) and in depth studies of problems identified in phase 1
Outcome	Initial report and concept for phase 2 *or* Assessment Report and policy recommendations	In-depth report discussed with stakeholders, terms of references for a series of follow-up activities to implement key recommendations

Source: Authors.

For example, phase 1 only requires the government of the country being assessed to approve the assessment, and participation by government officials is limited to interviews and some field visits with agencies involved in supporting and regulating trade and logistics. Phase 2 requires a greater commitment from the government: time and the resources (such as a steering committee) to organize the assessment, evaluate the various initiatives identified during its implementation, and organize follow-up activities.

Ideally, a TTFA will include both phases. But in some situations a decision can be made to not conduct the second phase. This will be the case when the primary deliverable of the assessment is a chapter in a larger economic report, or when the results of the first phase are inconclusive and the government lacks interest and funding to pursue additional activities.[5]

A single-phase assessment may be sufficient for smaller countries with relatively simple trading patterns. Although it is possible to decide in advance to limit a TTFA to a single phase, this toolkit recommends that this decision be made at the end of phase 1. If the country government decides not to continue to phase 2, additional phase 1 interviews can be performed to provide sufficient information on specific impediments or initiatives proposed to overcome these obstacles.

During phase 2—usually required for more sophisticated trading environments, such as emerging economies with a variety of markets and export supply chains—in-depth technical studies may be conducted to provide more detailed information on specific impediments that were identified and given priority during phase 1.

Notes

[1] See table C.1 (appendix C) for further details on how to map specific impediments into policy areas and project components.

[2] See appendix B for a detailed checklist of topics, participants, and activities needed to design specific project components.

[3] In general, projects need to balance the goal of promoting competition with the need to integrate services in the domestic market and offer scale in the international market.

[4] See box C.1 (appendix C) for a list of all policy areas covered in the assessment.

[5] This is also the case when the security environment does not permit a wider investigation.

CHAPTER 3

Overview of the Assessment's Analytical Structure and Key Transactions in the Trade Supply Chain

The logical framework to implement the assessment is to look at the supply chains linking a producer and a market, eventually distinguishing between different types of trades or commodities. The activities in the supply chain consist of a sequence of transactions between parties, logistics services, owner of the goods, regulatory agencies, banks, and infrastructure operators. The transactions may involve exchange of information, processing of documents, payments, and of course physical movement of goods.

Provided separately or in sequential combinations, logistics services include transport, consolidation, and storage of goods moving through a supply chain, as well as value-added services, such as assembly and customization, packaging, labeling, repair, and replacement. Regulatory activities include customs inspections and laboratory tests. (See figure 2.2 for a sample supply chain diagram, showing the services for a typical international supply chain connecting producers of exports with retailers selling imports.[1])

The goods moving through the supply chain may remain under the ownership of the exporter or importer or may be transferred between intermediaries along the way. So, transactions associated with each link in the supply chain may include the exchange of documents, payments, or information among the participants.

Participants in transactions can be grouped into four categories: cargo owners or traders (buyers and sellers), logistics services providers (freight forwarders, brokers, transport operators, multimodal facility operators (for example, ports)), financial intermediaries, and public agencies. Appendix A presents the basic components of different types of transactions: payments, documents used during the transaction, and information exchanged during it. Documents are used to place and confirm orders, initiate and confirm payments for goods and logistics services, certify the type and origin of goods, record changes in ownership and liability for goods while they are moving through the supply chain, and to show they comply with regulatory requirements. Information exchanged during transactions can include data on the location and status of goods within the supply chain, adjustments to production schedules and inventory, and the schedule and interface of sequential activities.

The TTFA brings knowledge on performance and bottlenecks by interviewing each side of key transactions in the supply chain. A typical interviewee will be part of several transactions with different counterparts. It is therefore essential that the team performing the assessment plan and conduct the interviews so as to cover well the transactions and physical movement of goods involved in the particular trades being assessed. However given the complexity of interaction and the scheduling constraints, the sequence of interviews is unlikely to follow that of the supply chain.

Phase 1

The first phase of the assessment is intended to provide an understanding of the quality of logistics services, physical and procedural bottlenecks, and how both contribute to competitiveness in international trade. Through direct interviews and feedback from participants in the international supply chains, phase 1 identifies activities and transactions that create bottlenecks and have the greatest impact on a country's or region's trade competitiveness. This phase 1s expected to require about six weeks to complete if there are no delays (figure 2.1).

Review and research. Phase 1 begins with reviewing the assessment's objectives and the concerns that led to the decision to conduct it. This is followed by desk research to identify the country's principal trades and previous studies on problems in the quality of transport and logistics services.

Selecting types of trade or type of consignment to study. At this point, the investigators should decide which types of cargo (defined by commodity group and direction of trade) to include in the assessment, basing this decision on the results of the desk research, the objectives of the assessment, and discussions with government. Making this decision early in the process is necessary because the competitive factors to be analyzed differ according to the type of cargo, as does the choice of logistics services.[2]

Interviews. Following the selection of cargo types, the investigators should arrange a series of meetings with associations and selected companies involved in these trades and related logistics services. The meetings should be open-ended and organized around the policy areas and topics covered by the assessment. Investigators should also arrange meetings with development agencies to discuss their specific concerns about trade facilitation.

Preliminary report. The initial output of phase 1 should be a draft report that presents the findings from the desk research and meetings in the field, including a discussion of the most important impediments identified, and the policy changes needed to address them. The report should also suggest future projects to realize opportunities to remove the trade impediments, plus a plan for conducting phase 2 of the assessment to obtain the information needed to design these projects.

Phase 2 planning or final policy note. Following the submission of the phase 1 draft report, the management of the entity commissioning the report should decide whether to move to an in-depth phase 2 assessment. This decision should be based on the substance of the initial findings but also on whether the government has sufficient interest to develop a trade facilitation project. If so, planning for phase 2 of the assessment should begin as early as possible. If the government decides not to continue to phase 2, investigators should prepare a final policy note with sufficient detail to support a policy dialogue and guide additional analytical work.

Phase 2

The second phase of the assessment provides information needed to design initiatives to improve the supply chain performance and estimate its benefits in terms of trade competitiveness.

Steering committee. Phase 2 implies a higher degree of participation of public and private stakeholders in the preparation of the assessment, its implementation and above all the preparation of the action plan that follows. It is therefore strongly recommended that the main focal point in the government organizes a steering committee that includes both public and private sector members. Key expected participants in the steering committee include transport agencies, customs, and commerce, with one agency being most likely the focal point for the assessment. Other participants include ministries of industry, infrastructure, planning, the central bank, business associations, freight forwarders' associations, and shippers' councils. The steering committee is expected to bring maximum ownership, facilitate access to information to the team of investigators, and increase relevance and implementability of the plans of action.

Selecting trades for supply chain analysis. Over the last two decades, a substantial portion of the effort to increase trade competitiveness has been directed at adding value in the supply chain. For this reason, the second phase of the assessment examines specific trades and their supply chains, defined in terms of their foreign and domestic origins or destinations and modes of international shipment.[3] The assessment examines both activities and transactions made throughout the supply chain. Logistics services and government regulations contribute to supply chain performance equally, and are directly associated with the movement and storage of goods, any intermediate processing, financial flows, and the exchange of information among participants in the supply chain.

Because of the breadth of the issues covered in an assessment, it is not possible to conduct sufficient interviews to generate statistically reliable data on the performance of individual services and transactions, or on the overall performance of the supply chains for the major commodities. To obtain more precise information on logistics activities, services, regulatory processes, and transactions, investigators must limit the assessment sample to the supply chains for specific trades. For larger countries, the sample may have to be further limited to a specific domestic geographic area, in the form of a few trade corridors or catchment areas. These limits are necessary to ensure that the information collected can be extrapolated and serves the objectives of the assessment.

Interviews. The interviews conducted during the phase 2 assessment should be open-ended and cover the same general topics as in phase 1, but in greater detail.[4] They should be sequenced to replicate flows in the supply chain to allow for follow-up questions concerning impediments to trade identified the interviewees. During the interviews, respondents should provide subjective rankings for the importance of these impediments, as well as some numeric data (such as time and cost) for use in validating these rankings.

Site visits. Interviews should be complemented with site visits to important facilities such as ports, border crossings, inland clearance facilities, and special zones to provide a better understanding of the flow of activities, the quality of the infrastructure, and the logic of the sequence of activities. Site visits should also allow verification of the interviewees' observations about the efficiency and effectiveness of the activities.[5]

Assessment report. The findings from the interviews, site visits, and analysis of sample data should be presented in an assessment report that also contains a detailed description of possible components of a trade facilitation project to address the impediments identified in the report. Before finalizing this report, the assessment team should conduct a stakeholders' workshop to present the results of the investigation and the proposed initiatives. The workshop is intended to assess support for these initiatives and the expected impact of their successful implementation, as well as to increase awareness and develop support for initiatives that will require both public and private participation.

Timeframe. The time and resources required for an assessment will vary with the scope as well as with the size of the economy and the geographical area being assessed. The total time required to conduct the assessment between effective launch of the assessment and draft report will be six to nine months. "Effective launch" means the first meeting between the team of investigators and a steering committee. This launch might be delayed when government needs time to mobilize public and private stakeholders, form a steering committee, and consult with them on the terms of reference.

Additional component studies (optional). If the phase 1 preliminary report highlights a problem that had been the focus of earlier investigations, and the government and task manager agree that a project is needed to address this problem, then a separate, in-depth project preparation study can be conducted during phase 2. The purpose of this study should be to design either a stand-alone project or a component of a trade facilitation project to address the problem. A component of a larger trade facilitation project could include other project components identified in phase 2 as well. The terms of reference for any in-depth studies should be prepared at the same time as the assessment team is preparing for the phase 2 interviews.

For example, a prefeasibility study to determine the current system for integration of automation at key gateways might be inspired by earlier studies of cargo clearance procedures that had identified the need for greater use of information technology (IT). Such as study should also focus on the inadequacies of the current system, identify project components to improve the use of IT, and provide a cost-benefit analysis of these components.

Another type of in-depth study might be useful in a case where problems of excessive costs or delays at a major gateway had already been identified in earlier transport studies and confirmed during the phase 1 meetings. The in-depth study would analyze the flow of cargo and the performance of individual operations and transactions to develop corrective measures for that gateway. The study report would offer a framework for implementing these measures, including a budget of the resources and time required.

The phase 2 assessment may also be complemented by data oriented activities. One example is the implementation of surveys with chambers of commerce of business associations: truckers' surveys and shippers' surveys.

Conducting the Assessment

The TTFA can be conducted in one or two phases (figure 3.1). This section describes the logistics of implementing a one- or two-phase assessment.

Phase 1

The purpose of phase 1 is to provide an understanding of the quality of logistics services, physical and procedural bottlenecks, and how both contribute to competitiveness in international trade. Therefore, phase 1 activities include:

- preparing a clear statement of the goals of the assessment
- performing desk research on the country's trade and freight logistics
- selecting commodities or type of consignment to be the focus of the assessment
- scheduling interviews with various associations and selected companies involved in these trades and related logistics services
- preparation of the initial report
- assisting in deciding whether the assessment should be continued to the next phase, and scope of work of the phase 2 assessment.

The phase 1 assessment requires the following personnel:

- task manager
- international logistics expert
- researcher
- local logistics consultant familiar with the country's trade and freight logistics.

Timeframe

Phase 1 is expected to require six to eight weeks to complete, including a one-and-a-half- to two-week visit to the country to conduct the interviews.

Defining Objectives

An important step in a TTFA is to develop a definition of the goal and objectives of the assessment. Though some assessments may be conducted primarily to provide information, the goals of most will be to provide a trade competitiveness diagnosis to inform country economic policies or to develop action and reform plans. The more specific the objectives, the more likely that the assessment will produce policies and projects that can address specific challenges. The objectives should be refined in discussions between the task manager and the broader team involved in working with the government, which commissioned the assessment.

Figure 3.1 Assessment Flowchart

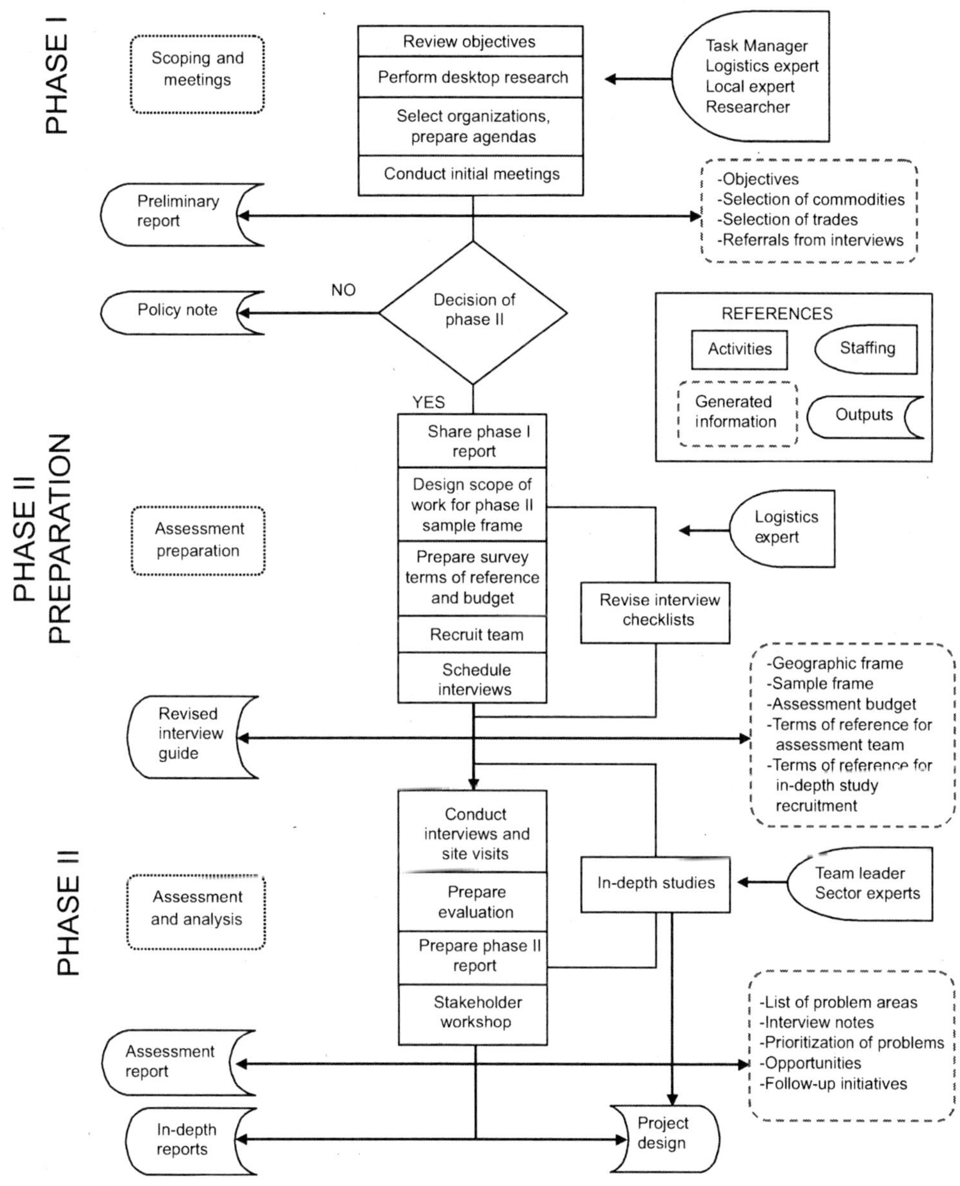

Source: Authors.

No matter how specific the objectives are, it is necessary to choose a limited set of commodities or cargoes and directions of trade on which the assessment will focus. Investigators can define the commodity groups with varying degrees of specificity, (for example, more generally as manufactured goods, or more precisely as wooden furniture), by the form in which cargo is transported (such as containerized, break bulk, or dry bulk), or by the type of cargo movement (such as perishables, bagged, bundled, or project).

It is especially important to distinguish trades according to the direction of flow—imports, exports, re-exports, and transit—because of differences in regulations and enforcement procedures. The default set should be exports of manufactured goods by container shipping. Imports are equally important, but because their distribution networks can be quite diverse, a narrower definition of the study set may be required. Despite this difficulty, the assessment should pay special attention to imports because they usually face tighter controls and greater delays (such as multiple inspections and delays in border crossing). Including air and rail shipments will require an increase in the resources used for the assessment, so they should be included only if they represent a substantial amount of the selected trades.

For example, a set of commodity groups chosen for an assessment might include containerized imports of consumer goods and equipment, exports of perishable goods requiring cold chains, consolidated shipments of manufactured exports, or high-valued cargoes shipped primarily by air. Investigators might also need to consider more complex supply chains because it is becoming increasingly common for certain industries to combine imported parts and components for assembly and later export.

Performing Desk Research

After the objectives of the assessment have been identified, a desk study should collect background information on the country's trade, major trade corridors, and principal gateways (see appendix E for details). This information, gathered from both published reports and Internet searches (box 3.1), should be used to:

- narrow the scope of the assessment
- but also provide confidence that any results can be extrapolated to a significant portion of the country's trade.

This research should also review background data from World Bank and regional bank projects in the transport and logistics sector. These projects promote customs modernization, road or rail corridor facilitation, port investments, private sector development, and export promotion. Because trade facilitation has been a popular topic in recent years, there are a number of customs reforms projects with a significant amount of information on both trade and clearance procedures. Also, consultants' reports used to prepare initiatives in trade facilitation and infrastructure development will contain performance data as well as insights on the more important impediments to trade facilitation. When collecting performance measurement data, it is important to check the accuracy of this information, using consultants' reports or other available source, because in many instances the primary data gathered may be inaccurate or misleading.

The desk research should produce contact information for organizations and enterprises active in trade and logistics that could be contacted for meetings during phase 1 of the assessment, and for interviews during phase 2. This list of potential contacts should include associations, such as shippers' councils and chambers of commerce and industry, and enterprises, such as major exporters and importers, international forwarders, integrators with a large domestic presence, and a major domestic road transporter.

Box 3.1. Data Sources

Data on the structure of foreign trade (the major commodities traded), the principal overseas origins and destinations, and the amount shipped is readily available from national trade statistics as well as international compilations such as those available through the International Trade Centre database and systems such as COMTRADE's WITS and TradeMap (see table E.1, appendix E). This information should be supplemented with information obtained during subsequent interviews with the ministry of trade or commerce and the local exporters association. These meetings should identify the principal trade routes and the competitive factors affecting the volume of trade.

Data on the level of activity at the major international gateways is usually available in the annual reports of the responsible authorities. Additional information is available from the publications of Lloyds, Drewry Shipping Consultants, International Air Transport Association (IATA), Airports Council International (ACI), and the United Nations Conference on Trade and Development (UNCTAD), among others. More detailed information can be obtained during interviews with the managers of the larger terminals, but these are not normally conducted until phase 2 of the Assessment. Collecting information on activity at the land borders presents a bigger challenge because very little data is published. In recent years, some regional and country studies prepared by the World Bank, African Development Bank (AfDB), United States Agency for International Development (USAID), and others have included information on the primary border crossings, but traffic data remains limited. Additional information can be obtained through subsequent interviews with customs officials, but their traffic data is usually limited to the value of goods crossing the border and is often inaccurate for land borders. Most traffic data will have to be obtained during interviews conducted at the border facilities. Data on border crossing times can be obtained from the International Road Transport Union for trucks making transit movements using TIR Carnets.

Data on the performance of the logistics sector can be obtained from various published indices, including the Logistics Performance Index and the data from the Doing Business survey, both maintained by the Word Bank and available through its Web site. Related indices include the Shipping Connectivity Index produced by UNCTAD and the Global Competitiveness Index maintained by the World Economic Forum.

Source: Authors.

Timeframe. Tasks related to desk research should require about two weeks of a researcher's time.

Selecting Organizations and Preparing Meeting Agendas

Following the desk research, the task manager, international logistics expert, and local logistics expert should select the commodities or cargoes and direction of trade on which the assessment will focus. Next, they should arrange meetings with:

- associations that represent enterprises involved in trade and freight logistics for these commodities or cargoes
- key companies (traders, freight forwarders)
- government agencies responsible for overseeing these enterprises and their trade
- multilateral and bilateral development organizations actively involved in trade promotion, trade facilitation, and development of international gateways or technical assistance for the trade and logistics sectors.

Table 3.1 shows a typical allocation of meetings and interviews among groups.

Table 3.1. Number of Meetings in Phase 1

Initial meetings	Number	Participants
Associations, chamber of commerce	5–6	Board members, most active member
Regulatory agencies	2–4	Directors, deputy commissioner, assistant secretary
Development agencies	1–3	Project staff
Border agencies	1–3	Director general, facility manager
Facility visit	1-3	Facility manager
Transport infrastructure operators	n.s.	Operations manager
Freight forwarders	n.s.	Branch manager
Road transport operators	n.s.	General manager
Exporters-importers	n.s	General managers, supply chain manager
Total	**10–19**	

Source: Authors.
n.s. = Not significant.

These associations and agencies should be selected from (but not limited to) the standard list in table G.3 (appendix G). Some will have been identified through the desk research, but the country office, the local logistics consultant, local businessmen, and academics should also provide guidance in selecting specific associations and organizations.

To limit the number of meetings, investigators can prioritize selectees using three criteria: size, effectiveness, and accessibility. For associations, the primary criterion should be to select organizations that are perceived as dynamic and representative of their industry. For agencies, the criteria should be effectiveness and accessibility. Relevant agencies are those that are active in setting policy and enforcing regulations that affect trade and transport. Bureaucratic agencies usually are more difficult to access, generally a good indication that they have little to contribute.

The meetings should be complemented by interviews with representatives of large companies involved in trade and logistics, covering the same topics but focusing on how the identified challenges affect their day-to-day operations. These companies should include two major importers or exporters, one or two international forwarders with a large presence in the country, and a major road transporter. These interviews should provide an understanding of the quality and variety of available logistics services and of the impact of government regulation on these services and on trade competitiveness.

To maximize the information obtained from each meeting, the investigators should send participants an agenda in advance, using the list of topics and subjects given in the first section of this toolkit's Interview Guide. The investigators should check this list of topics to be sure it is consistent with the selected commodities or cargoes, the information obtained from the desk research, and any insights provided by the assessment staff and local expert consultant. The agenda should be sent with a request that several persons familiar with the issues listed in the agenda attend the meeting.[6] For business associations, the participants should include members of the board or other active members. For government agencies, they should include senior officials responsible for both policy and operations. For example, in the meeting with customs representatives, the officers attending should have responsibility for general policy, legal, information technology, and risk management (see table 3.1 for an indicative list of participants). See appendix F for further details about preparing and executing phase 1 meetings.

Conducting Initial Meetings

The meetings should be conducted as open-ended discussions of the issues listed in the agenda to identify specific impediments to the performance of the logistics sector, as well as opportunities for facilitating trade. At the conclusion of the discussion, the investigators, and the meeting participants should review the relative importance of the impediments within each policy area.[7] For impediments already discussed during the meeting, the investigators should ask the participants if they feel that their impact on freight logistics is very important, significant, or marginal. For impediments not discussed, investigators should ask if they are substantial impediments and if the participants are familiar with this topic of trade logistics.

If it is anticipated that the assessment will continue into phase 2, then meeting participants should be asked to provide references for company executives and government officials who should be interviewed in the next phase.

Timeframe. Conducting the meetings should require about nine days: one day for organizing the meetings,[8] seven days for meetings and site visits, and one day for summarizing the results. This schedule assumes that international and local logistics experts will attend most meetings in pairs or with the assessment's task manager, with an average of three meetings per day.

Preliminary Report and Policy Note

The results of the desk research and initial meetings should be used to prepare a brief preliminary report summarizing the findings (see appendix C for a report outline). This report should describe:

- the structure of the most important trades and the general configuration of their supply chains
- the main impediments to growth of these trades and of logistics services
- opportunities for overcoming these impediments through changes in policy and public investments
- potential benefits to the quality of logistics services and trade competitiveness from making these changes.

The preliminary report should also comment on the potential for developing a trade facilitation project to build on these opportunities, and on the benefits of continuing to the second phase of the assessment.

Timeframe. Table 3.2 shows the staff resources required to complete phase 1, assuming 10–19 meetings. The additional resources required to prepare a policy note would depend on the scope and detail required, as well as any follow-up meetings or interviews. These follow-up meetings or interviews should not require more than two person-weeks.[9]

Table 3.2. Personnel Budget—Phase 1 (person days)

Task	Task manager	Researcher	Logistics expert	Local consultant	Admin. assist.
Planning supervision	5		1		3
Desk research		12			
Training, editing forms			3	1	1
Setting up meetings				1	3
Initial meetings	7		6	5	
Preliminary report	1		2		
Total	**13**	**12**	**12**	**7**	**7**

Source: Authors.

Phase 2—Preparation

Phase 2 preparation should include two sets of activities. The first set of activities should:

- organize a steering committee
- prepare a selection frame
- formulate an assessment plan.

The steering committee should include participants from the public and private sectors. The selection frame should specify the geographic area in which the interviews will be conducted, the trades to be examined, the type of organizations to be interviewed, and the number of interviews for each category.[10] The assessment plan should include a cost and time budget for these interviews and subsequent analysis of them, as well as an implementation plan and timeline (see Figure 3.1 for activities in a phase 2 assessment). Preparing the assessment plan is expected to require three to four weeks.

The second set of activities in phase 2 preparation should:

- organize the assessment team
- organize the interviews.

The assessment team should include a logistics expert as team leader and supporting members knowledgeable about the country's logistics sector and different supply chain activities and transactions. At this stage, the task manager should prepare terms of reference for the assessment team.

To organize the interviews, the assessment team should prepare a list of potential organizations to be interviewed and sites to be visited, as well as revise the interview guide by selecting topics from the pro forma checklists in the Interview Guide. The interview guide should include topics relevant to the selected trades that can be covered in little over an hour.

Timeframe. The minimum time required to complete phase 1 will be about six or seven weeks. During the execution of phase 2, the interviews with enterprises and agencies involved in the selected trades should require two to three weeks, depending on the number of interviews, size of the team, and difficulties in arranging the interviews. Analysis of the results from the interviews and preparation of the assessment report summarizing the findings and recommendations should require another two to three weeks. Therefore, the minimum time required for phase 2 should be three to four months.

Organizing a Steering Committee

The focal government agencies of the study should organize a steering committee with membership and objective as described above. The focal agency should build consensus in the committee, and especially act as secretariat not overlapping with administrative responsibilities of other key agencies. If preferable the committee might report to a non-stakeholding agency (prime minister, minister of finance). The committee is expected to intervene at the following stages:

- endorsement of the work program of the assessment
- presentation of intermediate reports
- discussion and endorsement of final report
- preparation of the plan of actions.

Since the assessment team includes seasoned international experts, the committee has also a capacity-building—if not training—role, bringing in global expertise to key policy makers in the country in an informal setting. The presentation of the intermediate or draft report also brings the opportunity to hold a series of workshops. These opportunities should be identified upfront as much as possible.

Preparing the Selection Frame

Because of the breadth of the assessment, the investigators should use a selection frame to select respondents with sufficient experience in trade and logistics (see appendix J for a sample frame and detailed discussion of selection frame components). To begin, the commodities or cargoes and direction of trade selected during phase 1 should be converted to specific trades that will serve as the focus of the interviews. A trade is defined by the commodity or cargo, foreign origin or destination, and primary mode of international transport used (see tables G.1 and G.2 in appendix G for further details about selecting specific trades).

The selection frame will include the shippers, consignees, and participants in the supply chains for these trades. The general structure of these supply chains, identified during phase 1, can be used to develop the frame. More specific information acquired during the phase 2 interviews may lead to some adjustment in the selection frame as phase 2 execution continues.

To ensure efficient use of assessment resources, the selection frame should also specify the area of the country in which the interviews will be conducted. Because the selected commodities or products for detailed study may be concentrated in a certain part of the country, the area should be chosen so that observations from the interviews can be representative of the problems of the country or the region. The best approach is to select a few major freight corridors and limit the assessment to only one of them when they are located far apart, in order to balance coverage and additional travelling and staffing costs. For larger countries—such as China, India, the Russian Federation, and Brazil—it is important to select at least two freight corridors serving different regions of the country.

Once the trade and geographic area have been selected, the selection frame should specify the categories of enterprises and public agencies to be interviewed, along with the position of the appropriate persons to be contacted. The initial list would be developed from information collected during the desk research and referrals obtained during phase 1. Finally, the number of interviews in each category can be determined based on the available time and resources. Once the selection frame is complete, individual enterprises and agencies can be chosen (see appendix J on the various factors for choosing them).

Budgeting Assessment Resources

The task manager and international logistics expert should prepare an initial estimate of the number of interviews to be conducted based on the selection frame and the objectives of the assessment. If the interviews are to be conducted in different areas of the country, the number of interviews for each area should be indicated. The task manager should use this estimate to prepare staffing and travel budgets. The resulting budget estimate should be compared with the available funding and, if necessary, the number of interviews should be adjusted. Because the actual number of interviews will change as a better understanding of the supply chains emerges from the meetings, the estimate should provide for extra interviews.

Because of the need to simultaneously conduct the interview and record the answers, two team members will need to attend the more challenging interviews—between one third to two thirds of the interviews. The average number of interviews that can be scheduled per individual team member per day will vary by country, assuming that a typical interview lasts about one and a half hours. If the average travel time between meetings is moderate—about 30–45 minutes—a reasonable average is three meetings per day.

In smaller countries with a relatively concentrated transport and logistics community and short travel times, it may be possible to average four interviews per day. In more difficult situations, where local movements are time-consuming or the process of setting up meetings is very formal, the average may drop to as low as two interviews per day. To this schedule must be added the time for site visits, as well as for travel between cities if required by the geographical coverage.

With an average of three interviews per day—about half involving two team members—the interviews for the sample size shown in table 3.3 would require 17–28 person days. Site visits are assumed to add three to four person days, assuming that each visit involves only one team member. To these must be added the time required for organizing interviews, ad hoc meetings, and unexpected delays. The resulting level of effort should be six to seven person-weeks. For a larger sample size, a geographic area covering multiple cities, or more difficult movements within a city, this level of effort could increase by half.

A complete personnel budget (table 3.4) should include not only the activities of the task manager and the technical experts but also the local administrative assistant who arranges the interviews. The time required for analysis and report preparation can be significant, because this work will require interpretation rather than a simple statistical analysis. (The assessment team leader should have primary responsibility for writing the assessment report.) The budget should also include travel time for foreign experts and for local travel if the assessment covers a large geographical area.

Table 3.3. Sample List of Interviews

Groups interviewed	Number of interviews
Exporters/importers	6–12
Freight forwarders, integrators	4–8
Consolidator, distribution center	2–3
Customs broker	2–4
Road transport companies	4–8
National railways	1
Shipping lines	2–3
Cargo airlines	2–3
Port terminal	1–2
Airport cargo terminal	2
Free zone, dry port	1–2
Banking institutions	2
Unscheduled interviews	3–4
Subtotal	32–54
Customs facilities	2
Other government agencies	5–6
Total	**39–62**

Source: Authors.

The personnel budget estimate in table 3.4 does not include the time required for any in-depth studies. Although the level of effort for these studies will depend on the nature of the impediments and solutions being analyzed, they should be designed to be completed at the same time as the rest of phase 2, about two months following the start of the preparation stage.

Table 3.4. Personnel Budget—Phase 2 (person days)

Task	Task manager	Logistics expert	Technical experts	Admin. assist.
Phase 2—preparation				
Preparing sample frame	1	2		
Editing interview checklists		3		
Budget and interview list	1	3		
Terms of reference and recruitment	2	3		
Phase 2—execution				
Planning supervision	3		3	
Interviews and site visits	4		30	
Analysis	1		5	
Report preparation	2		8	2
Travel	2		4	
Total	**16**	**11**	**50**	**2**

Source: Authors.

Reviewing Interview Checklists

Once the selection frame is completed, the budget finalized, and a list of enterprises to be interviewed is established, the interview forms and the terms of reference for the assessment team should be prepared.

The interviews should be open-ended, but with more structure than the meetings in phase 1. Accordingly, the interview forms should contain a checklist of topics that should guide the interview, leaving the interviewers the freedom to ask their own questions. This freedom requires interviewers to be knowledgeable about freight logistics and trade facilitation and have previous training in the assessment procedures.

The Interview Guide in this toolkit includes pro forma checklists for each category of respondent (see appendix G for a list of the general topics covered by the checklists). Appendix D contains additional information mapping the topics and respondents involved in each policy area. But to ensure that the interview can be completed in one and a half hours, the toolkit interview lists must be reviewed and shortened before the interview. Topics not relevant to the objectives of the assessment or inapplicable to the country should be excluded, based on the findings from the phase 1 meetings.[11] These could include subjects that are:

- not relevant to the trades being assessed
- unfamiliar to the respondent
- already covered in sufficient detail during the initial phase 1 interviews.

For an interview to be manageable, the edited checklists should include no more than 20–25 topics, assuming that each topic requires an average of three to four minutes. But as the assessment progresses and additional impediments to supply chain performance are identified, new topics will be added to the interview forms (see table 3.5 for an example of this process). No matter how many new topics are added, it is important to retain the topics in the initial interview form so that the responses of all participants can be compared, and to limit the number of new topics added to keep the interview length within one and a half hours.

Table 3.5. Sample Process of Adding Items to the Interview Checklist

Customs	Transport	Exporter
Initial item		
Average clearance times	**Typical load factors**	**Sensitivity to order time**
Item added sequentially in response to new information		
• Proportion requiring more than "x" days • Delays due to documentation or payment • Delays at discretion of consignee	• Level of competition • Opportunities to consolidate loads • Mechanisms for securing backhauls	• Problem in production or delivery time • Initial orders versus replenishment • Fluctuation-total order or mix of (Stock Keeping Unit)

Source: Authors.

Recruiting Assessment Personnel

The assessment team should normally include three to six experts, depending on the assessment's scope and deadlines, including technical experts familiar with transport, regulatory requirements, and supply chain management. Where possible, they should be locally hired. (See appendix H for sample terms of reference for assessment team members.)

The selection of a leader for the assessment team is critical, because this individual will be responsible not only for supervising the interviews and analyzing the results but also for preparing the assessment report. The team leader should have several years of international experience in evaluating transport and logistics services[12] and be familiar with supply chain analysis and the techniques for integrating supply chains. Experience in conducting assessments or similar efforts and familiarity with the procedures described in this toolkit are essential. The World Bank is in the process of developing a list of qualified personnel and plans to provide training in assessment procedures to expand this list.

Despite the formal structure outlined in this toolkit, the TTFA relies on the perceptions of the assessment team. It is therefore essential to recruit a team with sufficient experience and analytical skills. Team members should be familiar with the logistics industry or otherwise involved in international trade and must have experience conducting interviews. Members may be seconded from logistics service providers or academics working in the area of transport and logistics, although scheduling their time is likely to be problematic.

Finally, the participation of local technical experts in the assessment team is important because they are knowledgeable about the local logistics industry, the principal users of third party logistics, and past efforts to modernize supply chains and improve regulatory processes. A technical expert should also be recruited for each in-depth study. In countries where sufficient candidates cannot be identified, experts may be recruited from the country's region, but this should be the exception.

Phase 2—Execution

Once preparations for phase 2 are complete, the team should begin interviewing the selected enterprises and government agencies. It is important that the enterprise or agency be informed of the purpose of the assessment and the general topics to be discussed, so that the persons attending are knowledgeable about these topics. At the beginning of the interview, the interviewer should explain that the information collected during the meeting is for the purpose of a general analysis and will not be attributed to the organization.

Conducting Interviews

The form and flow of the interview should be determined by the interviewer, with the checklist used to ensure that the relevant topics are covered and serve as a memory aid on the specific issues linked to each topic.

During the interview, the investigators should collect performance data on the logistics activity performed by the interviewee for each of the supply chains in which he or she is involved. Performance data should cover time and cost information for each part of the supply chain, disaggregating its most representative components. For example, time indicators would include port dwell time, delays in land border crossings, and customs and border agencies clearance times. Cost information should ideally cover the most important charges faced by firms participating in a particular supply chain (such as transportation costs per kilometer for all transport modes involved, bribes and informal payments, and other fees and surcharges paid to agents) and for alternative routes to the same market of origin or destination. Some measure of variation should be also gathered for typical and best-case scenarios, to roughly estimate reliability indicators for each part of the supply chain.

The last 20 minutes of the interview should be devoted to summarizing the major impediments to improving supply chain performance, the opportunities for overcoming these obstacles, and the likely impact if these opportunities were realized. The impediments should be ranked using a method similar to that used in phase 1.

In scheduling, the interviews should be sequenced to improve the quality of information. Respondents should be interviewed in the order they are sequential participants in the supply chain. This sequencing allows interviewers to cross-check observations from one participant in a supply chain with the other parties with whom he interacts.

For exports, the interview sequence should move down the supply chain, beginning with the producer of the goods, to understand how problems occurring in one component of the supply chain affect performance in subsequent components. For imports, the sequence should begin with the importer—usually a trader, wholesaler, or retailer—and move back through the supply chain to observe how adjustments are made at one stage to compensate for uncertainties in earlier ones. This sequence is also useful in obtaining referrals because one respondent can identify the other parties with whom he interacts.

Although it is difficult to schedule interviews in a specific order, every effort should be made to ensure correspondence of interviews with both parties to some of the key transactions—for example, the shippers and the forwarders, the customs brokers and the customs officials, the transport company and the gateway operator (see appendix A). Having the same team members attend both interviews will provide a better opportunity to compare observations by the two sets of interviewees. An example of these pairings is shown in table 3.6.

Table 3.6. Pairing Interviews for a Trade

Pairs of interviewees for key transactions	
Shippers	**Domestic transporters**
Port authority	Shipping lines
Airport authority	Airlines
Domestic transport	Consolidator
Forwarder	Clearance agent
Clearance agent	Customs
Forwarder	Warehousing
Shipper	Banks

Source: Authors.

Site visits should also be scheduled to important facilities such as ports, border crossings, inland clearance facilities, and special zones to provide a better understanding of the flow of activities, the quality of the infrastructure, and the logic of the sequence of activities.

Spontaneous interviews may occur during site visits, or ad hoc meetings may be arranged during scheduled interviews. To simplify the analysis, the information collected on these occasions should be classified into the same topics shown in appendix G. The assessment team may also schedule follow-up interviews to clarify specific issues and explore options for addressing specific impediments.

For those interviews that are expected to cover a broad range of activities and transactions, two members of the assessment team should be present, one to lead the interview and the other to take detailed notes. The assignment of team members to specific interviews, especially those conducted by only one member, should be based on each team member's area of expertise.

Evaluating Results

The results from the interviews will not provide a statistically reliable measure of opinion on problems in supply chain performance. Instead, they can determine if there is consensus on the importance of these impediments among medium to large firms involved in international trade. During the evaluation, a summary of the detailed notes from each interview should be shared with all members of the assessment team. The team should prepare a summary of common themes, including specific impediments, opportunities for overcoming them, and expected changes in supply chain performance. Expected changes may include not only improvements in the cost and time for moving goods but also improvements in the quality of individual logistics services and changes in the structure of international supply chains.

The assessment team should begin its evaluation of the interview results by compiling a list of the policy areas in which impediments were identified during the phase 1 meetings or phase 2 interviews (see table 3.7). Following this, the assessment team should prepare a more detailed list of these impediments based on their review of the interview notes and grouped under the same general policy area headings.[13] The assessment team should use this longer list to develop a ranking based on the frequency with which these specific impediments were mentioned and the importance given to them by the respondents. A key point to remember in conducting the analysis is that individual respondents will not be aware of some types of impediments—which can be accounted for by ranking them "not relevant."

Table 3.7. Intensity of Identified Impediments by Policy Areas (number of respondents)

Policy areas	Interviews: Very important	Interviews: Marginal	Interviews: Not relevant	Qualitative evaluation by assessment team
Tools and institutions to measure and assess logistics performance	7	25	2	. . .
Transport and infrastructure policies	11	15	3	3
Multilateral cooperation	5	24	6	2
Regional agreements and cooperation	16	15	4	3
Domestic institutions promoting trade and transport facilitation policies, mandating effectiveness and governance	12	23	2	4
Regulation of transport and logistics services	14	13	3	5
Quality, reliability of logistics services	6	32	0	5
Business practices	4	25	8	4
Customs modernization	5	24	6	4
Related procedures	16	15	4	3
Trade facilitation initiatives	11	15	3	4
Transit regime	4	26	8	5
Air and sea connectivity and liberalization of services	6	32	0	5
Public infrastructure	14	13	3	2
Enhancing competitiveness of key products supply chains	12	23	2	2

Source: Authors.

Following the prioritization of the impediments extracted from interviews knowledge, the team should also provide an expert assessment of the relative importance of each impediment based on the global expertise of its members. This evaluation should take into account the impact on supply chains of the identified impediments in time, cost, and reliability for the selected types of trades. For this purpose, a numeric scale from 1 (least impact) to 5 (most impact) can be used to confront the perception emerging from the interviews, with analytical understanding of the local supply chains. Although there is no systematic procedure to properly weight these two pieces of information, the assessment team should consider both when prioritizing project components—hence, striking a balance between the potential real impact of proposed components and the impediments which are most prevalent in the opinion of the interviewees.

Preparing a Plan of Actions

Finally, the team should work with the steering committee and the focal agency to prepare a plan of action describing the opportunities for improvement identified during the interviews and recommendations. Table C.1 (see appendix C) offers a basic framework for analyzing these impediments and translating them into remedial action through specific project components. Appendix B provides a conceptual map of the specific activities and participants involved in each component.

The summary should also include an assessment of the time required to implement the policy components it recommends (See table 3.8 for an example list of recommended policy components and their potential timeframe.) This data can then be combined with the perception of those interviewed to prioritize the impediments and evaluate the impact of the opportunities for improvements.

Table 3.8. Sample of Project Components to Improve Trade and Logistics Identified in the Assessment

Project component (by policy area)	Included measures	Time to implement (years)	Leading agency for the component
Overall project monitoring	Logistic council	1	Transport or Commerce
	Logistics observatory to monitor performance	1-2	
Customs modernization	Improvement in transit system	2	Customs
	Expand the Authorized Economic Operator Program	1-2	
	New information system	2	
Development of logistics zones	Master plan	1	Infrastructure/Industry
	New code for bonded warehouses	1-2	
	Revision of concession law	1-2	
	Development of sample TORs	1/2	

Source: Authors.

It is strongly recommended that the measures should be grouped in a limited number of project components that could be implemented by a project management unit with clear leadership and responsibilities. A typical TTFA should not lead to more than 10 to 15 component projects, each of which will be allocated the design and implementation of a series of measures, in the same policy areas, under clear leadership and accountability.

The team will work closely with the members of the steering committee to identify and propose a sustainable implementation strategy (box 3.2). The team and the stakeholders should also look at the relevance of an umbrella project to follow the overall implementation of the plan of actions, in the form of a logistics or a facilitation council.

The plan will propose appropriate measures for monitoring the impact of the projects and develop the mechanisms for collecting and evaluating the data used to produce these measures. This monitoring will target success indicators of component projects as well as tools such as "logistics observatories" that can help countries assess in details the change in their logistics performance.

Assembling the Draft Assessment Report

The final assessment report should summarize the results from both the meetings in phase 1 and the interviews in phase 2, including estimated cost, time, and reliability data, and diagrams of typical supply chains. (See appendix C for an outline for phase 1 and II reports.) In case complementary in-depth studies have been implemented as part of the phase 2 report (such as surveys or prefeasibility studies), the corresponding output should be summarized as chapters in the main report.

The report should also provide an implementation strategy for remedial action that could be included in a trade facilitation project or other trade and transport projects. The project description should include timeframe, composition, accountability, and leadership of the project team, and the outline of a work program for design and implementation of the measures in the scope of work.

Box 3.2. Organizing the Follow-Up Effort

The steering committee of the TTFA has a key role during the diagnostic phase that should lead the same group of policy makers and stakeholders into implementation. This group should participate with the expert team in outlining and evaluating potential initiatives, specifically the estimates of the time required for implementation and of the likelihood of a successful outcome. Time estimates should distinguish between short-term actions (less than six months), medium-term actions (up to two years), and long-term projects. The group should help identify any homogeneous subgroups potentially responsible for the design and implementation of measures in specific policy areas

Hence the steering committee at the end of the TTFA should evolve into a project structure hosting several specialized PMUs. This group should continue to be involved during the project design and implementation, but with some modification in the membership. The remaining and new members should be appropriate for the selected initiatives and should include private sector stakeholders. The group should direct the follow-up technical studies. The expert team has an important role of helping share international experience in the implementation of plans of action.

Source: Authors.

Holding the Stakeholders' Workshop

A stakeholders' workshop should be held once the draft final report is cleared by the steering committee and the review process by the agency implementing the assessment. The workshop should be a one-day meeting in which the assessment findings are presented, including opportunities for improving supply chain performance and trade competitiveness and initiatives proposed to realize these opportunities. This workshop should allow the assessment team to reach a wider audience and assess support for the proposed initiatives from the private sector as well as the government. The team should also be able to assess the changes in behavior to be expected if these initiatives were introduced. After this workshop, the team should prepare the final assessment report.

Follow-up Technical Studies

After the assessment is completed, the project implementation team can commission follow up technical studies to determine the scope, resource requirements, and benefits of each project component recommended in the final assessment report (figure 3.2). These studies may apply various types of analysis, including:[14]

- operations analysis and management studies
- legal and policy reviews
- design and feasibility studies
- needs assessment and benchmarking studies.

Figure 3.2. Technical and In-depth Studies for Designing Project Components

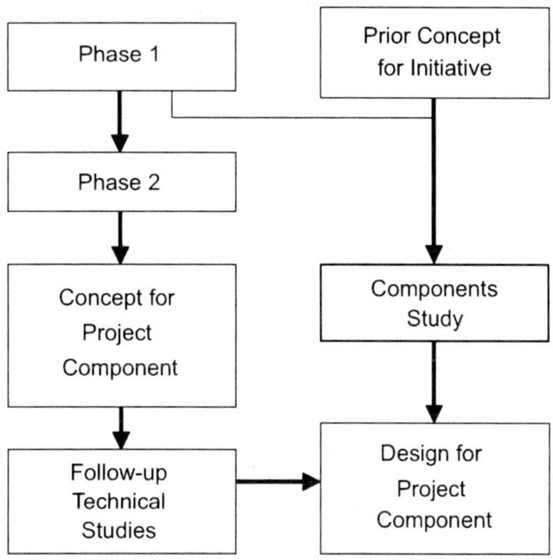

Source: Authors.

The technical study should also include an assessment of the role of public–private partnerships in implementing projects, such as the following:

- improvements in the quality of logistics services
- introduction of new technologies
- improvements in operation of public infrastructure
- development of trade-related clusters.

Typical Timeline of the Assessment

Figure 3.3 shows the timeline typically required to conduct an assessment. For an assessment limited to the first phase followed by preparation of a policy note, the estimated time is two and a half months. For a two-phase assessment, the time will increase to about six months. The six-month estimate assumes a continuous effort without significant downtime and minimal delays in administrative approval, including selection and mobilization of the interview team. A more likely timeframe would be seven to eight months, assuming delays in preparing for the interviews and a delay between completing the fieldwork and preparing the final assessment report. This timeframe should fit a wide range of sample sizes and geographical areas, because the greater amount of work needed for larger projects would be met by increasing the size of the assessment team.

Figure 3.3. Typical Timeline for a Trade and Transport Facilitation Assessment (months)

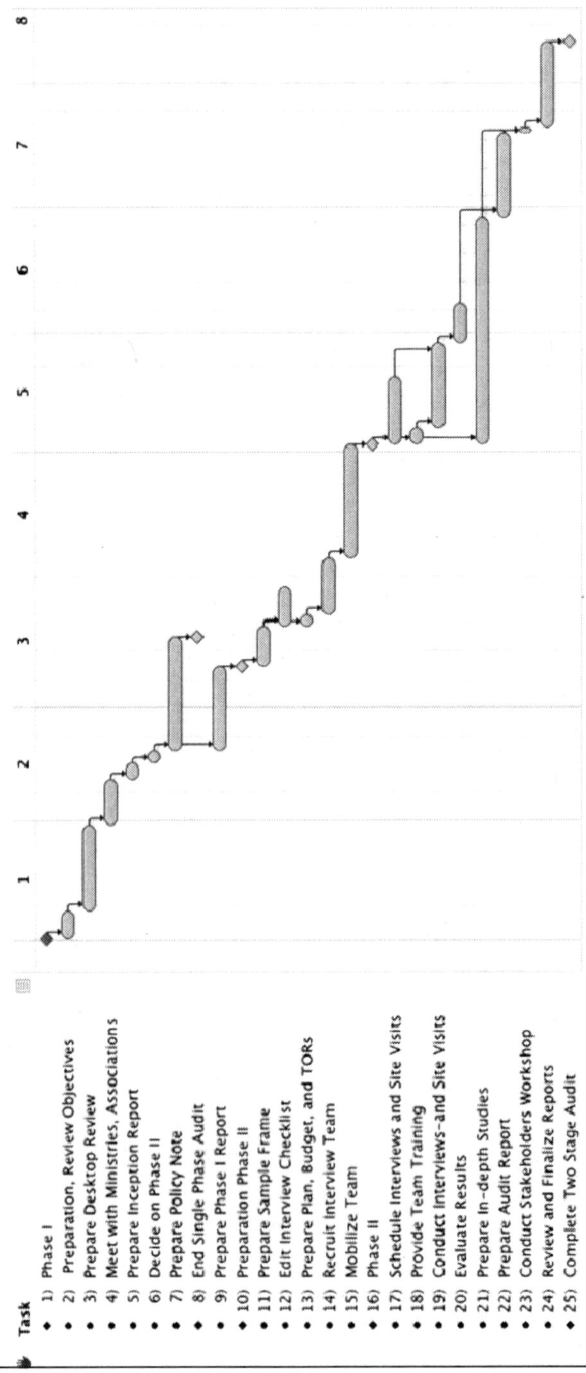

Source: Authors.

Notes

[1] This supply chain diagram assumes that the services are not integrated and that ownership is transferred only from the producer to the wholesaler and then to the retailer.
[2] For example, liquid and dry bulk cargoes have simple logistics organized by the producers. Unitized cargoes, which often include multiple consignments, have elaborate logistics organized by different parties in the supply chain.
[3] Questions that might be used to select the trades are shown in table G.2 (appendix G).
[4] Appendix G summarizes the information to be collected.
[5] These visits should be integrated with the interview, especially for customs clearance facilities and cargo handling operations.
[6] Specifying the desired expertise of the attendants helps to avoid meetings where the head of the association merely presents what the organization is doing.
[7] A simple scorecard can be used to rank impediments according to the respondent's perception: 0 = irrelevant/not an impediment; 1 = marginal impediment; 2 = significant impediment; 3 = very important impediment.
[8] Much of the organization will precede arrival in the country, but an additional day will be required to organize the logistics at the country level.
[9] See appendix H for sample terms of reference for the international and domestic logistics experts and the researcher.
[10] The total number of interviews will be limited by the budget allocated for this phase.
[11] For example, in countries where exporters sell ex factory and importers purchase for delivery to their warehouse, it is expected that these groups will have limited knowledge of activities at the gateway, and therefore should be excluded. In countries with clearing and forwarding agents, topics covering these two functions should be combined and there should be no separate interviews with customs clearance agents. In countries that require cargo to be cleared at the border, there should be no need for topics concerning internal transit or clearance. In countries that are within a customs union, topics regarding border crossings should either be modified or eliminated.
[12] Because this is a relatively new field, 5–10 years of experience is not unreasonable but should have been preceded by experience in related fields, such as transport and trade promotion or facilitation.
[13] Box C.1 (see appendix C) presents in greater detail the interview topics that relate to general policy areas or impediments shown in table 3.7.
[14] See appendix K for details about the analytical components of a typical technical study.

CHAPTER 4

Issues and Examples in Conducting a Trade and Transport Facilitation Assessment

Many government and development agencies have implemented the original Trade and Transport Facilitation Assessment (TTFA) toolkit, including the World Bank, which conducted about 50 assessments during 2001–08. These assessments can provide useful insights about the effects that different levels of government participation will have on the assessment or about common challenges in identifying supply chain bottlenecks.

Levels of Government Participation in Implementing Recommendations

Since the first edition of this toolkit, a large number of assessments have been initiated by development agencies as a service delivered to the governments of developing countries. Increasingly, assessments are being performed at the request of governments interested in improving the performance of their logistics sector and international supply chains. Governments have responded in a variety of ways to the project components recommended by these assessments.

Although the majority of recommended projects should be undertaken by the government, a significant subset requires cooperation between the government and the private sector.[1] This was the case in Morocco and Tunisia, where there was a high level of government commitment to improving freight logistics (box 4.1). Results were less substantial in the Central African Republic because of lower levels of government involvement, but the assessment still provided a basis for policy discussion and for development of regional initiatives (box 4.2).

Similarly limited government participation characterized the development of a regional project for the Mashreq countries (Syria, Jordan, and Lebanon). In this case, a phase 1 assessment provided the mechanism for starting the dialogue, and also helped to identify common concerns that could serve as the basis for design of the regional project. However, the dynamics of regional trade and the contributions of a regional corridor project would require a second phase of the assessment (box 4.3).

Box 4.1. Morocco and Tunisia: High Level of Government Involvement

The two Maghreb countries used different approaches in applying a variation of the Trade and Transport Facilitation Assessment very similar to a phase 2 assessment. In both cases the work was requested by the government and involved a high level of commitment. While the Moroccan assessment built on earlier trade facilitation projects, the Tunisian effort included complementary activities such as a shipper survey.

For Morocco, the assessment results indicated that the investment levels and quality of services in road transportation were very low and logistics advisory and consulting services and logistics platforms were almost unavailable. The costs and time required for exports and imports were too high—for exports because of no separation between freight and passenger traffic, for imports because of no coordination among the players and the absence of a port facilitation culture. The assessment also indicated that the clearance procedure application was relatively cumbersome, information management inefficient, and use of information technologies too low. Proposed projects aimed to increase the quality of road transport, reduce maritime costs and time of crossing with port facilitation measures, and decrease vulnerability to illegal activities. The action plan included promoting investment in logistics services and facilitating economic regimes applicable to logistic operations.

For Tunisia, the assessment found that the main supply chain impediments related to poor port capacity, almost nonexistent storage infrastructure, and limited and low-quality supply of transport services, especially trucking, as well as other impediments in customs clearance procedures. The assessment recommended capacity-building work directed to private agents and business organizations, upgrading logistics zones infrastructure through PPPs (public-private partnerships), and customs facilitation.

The Moroccan effort was implemented through a project management unit involved in the design and execution of the assessment, as well as designing the follow-up project components. With one exception, the government implemented these project components without the support of the World Bank. The Tunisian government was also involved in implementing the assessment and designing project components, later financed by the World Bank and the European Union.

Sources: World Bank, 2006; World Bank, 2008.

Box 4.2. Central African Republic: Low Level of Government Involvement

A relatively limited undertaking similar to a phase 1 assessment, the Central African Republic assessment was part of a Diagnostic Trade Integration Study, with the assessment information used to complement planning for transport investment projects. The assessment found that traders in the Central African Republic face high transit costs because of the distance to the nearest sea port, the cost of the return trip with empty containers, and very expensive transit procedures. In addition, infrastructure quality was found to be rather poor. The TTFA found that the logistics services offered were of a good quality, at prices comparable to those found in the European Union.

The assessment's recommendation to improve the transit regime lacked active government involvement and so did not result in the design of project components for trade facilitation. Instead, the results were used in developing a transit component for the Central Africa Trade Facilitation project and in estimating the logistics costs for that project's appraisal documents.

Source: World Bank, 2007.

Box 4.3. Mashreq: Regional Assessments

An early version of this Trade and Transport Facilitation Assessment was used to develop a regional project for the Mashreq countries. Phase 1 assessments conducted in Syria, Jordan, and Lebanon identified a common interest in improving the main freight corridors serving the region, particularly the north–south corridor linking Turkey to Saudi Arabia and the United Arab Emirates. Because the three countries were in the process of implementing the ASYCUDA customs information system, have signed bilateral arrangements allowing trucks to transport cargo to and from neighboring countries, and are members of the TIR system, implementing a regional transit regime seemed feasible.

But the assessment results indicated that related difficulties discouraged movement through the region. Site visits to the border crossings between Jordan and Syria revealed reasonably efficient operations, but the convoy system used for internal transit was slow and cumbersome. Interviews with the port operators indicated that conversion to private operations had improved performance, but volumes and shipping services were still limited. Liberalization of the financial transactions and access to foreign exchange had allowed an increase in formal trade, but some vestiges of the earlier system designed to bypass government taxation remained. There was adequate road transport capacity, but formal allocation of import shipments continued to limit the quality of service in Syria and Lebanon. Though Jordan had successfully modernized its trucking fleet, Syria and Lebanon had older, less reliable trucks, creating downward pressure on trucking rates.

These findings were used to develop a regional corridor project with components to address these problems and complement investments in infrastructure. Within six months of completing the assessments a project incorporating many of their proposals was under preparation.

Source: World Bank, 2009.

Identifying Bottlenecks in the Supply Chain—Challenges and Opportunities

One of the challenges investigators and governments face is to identify hidden bottlenecks that have a critical impact on trade competitiveness, while most of the impediments identified by stakeholders in the field may not have the same impact. The former tend to describe causes, the latter symptoms. This section examines the reasons why projects may fail to identify these causes within the supply chain.

First, international supply chains usually involve complex combinations of sequential activities. Poor performance in one part of a supply chain can propagate forward or backward, often reappearing as larger problems in other parts of the chain and leading to misdiagnosis of the cause of poor performance.[2] Operations research techniques have been used with some success to identify the causes of delay with sequential physical activities but are less effective when analyzing a series of transactions such as those found in a supply chain. Limiting the scope of analysis to physical activities overlooks important aspects of the transactions, specifically financial and regulatory elements (box 4.4).

Second, problems can appear significant within the context of a component of the supply chain but have relatively little impact on overall performance of that chain, thus diverting attention from needed reforms. One of the challenges when conducting an assessment is to maintain a broad perspective, because individual respondents usually have a narrow focus on those problems that are most irritating to performing their own tasks. To reduce this bias, the TTFA searches for consensus among the participants in the supply chain. Unfortunately, most respondents have limited knowledge of the activities in a supply chain other than those in which they are directly involved. When discussing these other problems, they usually express the prevailing opinion.[3] Only through careful cross-checking and supply chain analysis, using cost and time data collected during the interviews, can those problems having a truly significant effect on supply chain performance be identified (box 4.5).

Box 4.4. Syria: Financial and Regulatory Impediments

Until recently, Syria faced a series of substantial challenges to seamless logistics. Government restrictions on trucking services and customs brokers and on public monopolies in shipping agencies and ports prevented modernization of these activities. Heavy regulation of trade, including excessive documentation and cumbersome customs procedures, added to the difficulties faced by exporters.

However, a 2004 logistics assessment indicated that a major impediment to trade was the complex procedures for accessing foreign exchange. Although the government had only recently liberalized exchange control, shippers continued to use complex supply chains devised to avoid exchange controls. And freight forwarders still provided trade financing in an effort to circumvent the exchange controls and reduce taxes by avoiding reporting the value of transactions. A 2009 assessment revealed substantial improvement in trade facilitation, including removal of the exchange rate controls, privatization of the ports, and other reforms—all allowing shippers to develop more efficient supply chains. Nevertheless, the practice of relying on offshore financing continued to reduce exposure to taxes.

Source: World Bank, 2004.

Box 4.5. Central Africa: Respondent Perspectives

Several studies have identified poor road conditions, roadblocks, and border crossings as the most important impediments to efficient transport along corridors in Central Africa. But a recent study of cargo movements concluded that none of these were the major constraint on supply chain performance.

Roadblocks and maintenance problems created by poor road conditions are particularly annoying to drivers because they cannot be controlled. However, analysis of the time and costs for the various components of the supply chain concluded that roadblocks account for less than 10 percent of road transport costs (and an even smaller percentage of transit time, around 5 percent). Maintenance costs account for a larger percentage of trucking costs, but much less than fuel. More important, maintenance and tires costs mainly caused by poor road conditions were not a significant portion of total transport costs compared to fuel costs.

Although poor road conditions increase travel time, about 75 percent of total transit time is actually spent in port. Cumbersome procedures and shippers' strategies explain why seaports account for a significant portion of total logistics costs. However, the most important cost factor for transport in Central Africa is the premiums charged by the trucking cartel that enjoys the protection of bilateral transit quotas and queuing systems.

Source: CEMAC Transit and Transport Facilitation Project (2007). Project Appraisal Document, World Bank.

A third difficulty is the classic case of "blaming the messenger." Logistics services providers are often blamed for poor service quality in situations where they are merely responding to the demands of their clients (box 4.6). Continual efforts by shippers to reduce costs ultimately leads to problems such as overloaded trucks, poorly prepared shipping documents, misrepresentation of cargoes, and missed connections. Shippers' effect on supply chain performance is most obvious when they organize the supply chain but can be equally substantial when they only determine the terms of shipment. Regulatory agencies experience similar problems when asked by the government to improve enforcement without being provided with adequate resources. And they face the same obstacles when asked to quickly expand the scope of their activity without being given time to develop an effective implementation plan.[4]

Box 4.6. The Philippines: Shipping Strategies

An assessment of the logistics sector in the Philippines was prepared in 2003, followed by a strategic review of the transport sector in 2004. Both studies examined the corridor connecting the island groups of Mindanao and Luzon and the inability of agricultural products from Mindanao to compete with foreign imports in the major markets in Manila and Cebu cities. The transport review confirmed the inefficiency of the domestic port facilities, the lack of modern domestic shipping services, and the lack of competition throughout the supply chain. The review's recommendations for addressing these problems were well known but had never been implemented.

But the supply chain analysis revealed the lack of an organized agricultural sector in Mindanao, Philippines, with the result that both the volumes shipped and the size of shipments were relatively small. A reassessment of the transport services revealed that what had been perceived as inefficiencies were in fact adaptations to small consignments, and that improving competitiveness depended on introducing consolidation early in the supply chain.

Source: Arnold and Villareal (2002).

A final difficulty in separating symptoms from causes is the failure to examine the entire supply chain, including the international movement of goods. Though often neglected, a significant percentage of trade movement can take place outside of the country and contribute most of the transit time and cost along the supply chain (box 4.7).

Box 4.7. Nepal: Supply Chains Outside the Country

Several reviews have been prepared for the corridor connecting Kathmandu with the international ports near Calcutta, especially for shipments of containerizable cargo. Many reviews examined specific components of the corridor, most notably the roads and border crossings, which had received the most criticism. Roads were not well maintained and border crossings lacked infrastructure and transparent procedures. A review of the supply chain—part of a general study of subregional links in South Asia—revealed that, although these components did need improvement, they had relatively little impact on supply chains compared to the delays that cargo experienced in the international ports (outside Nepal) because of inefficient operations and the lack of scheduled services. These results suggest that, for European markets, a longer land route across India to Mumbai would reduce both time and costs for door-to-door movement.

A similar analysis was used in a subsequent study of the potential for shipping exports from Northeast India via the port of Chittagong in Bangladesh. In this case, the border crossing was more problematic, but even with an efficient border crossing procedure, the cost and time spent in the port made this an unattractive route.

Source: Subramanian and Arnold (2001).

Notes

[1] The stakeholders likely to be directly involved in these project components are listed in tables B.2 and B.3 (appendix B).

[2] For example, a requirement that truckers had to guarantee payment of duties before entering a neighboring country created long queues of vehicles exiting the country. This caused congestion on the road network and rent-seeking behavior by officials at the point of exit. In contrast, the neighboring country had an efficient, uncongested clearance operation.

[3] A common example is the tendency to blame customs for delays that are caused by other participants in the supply chain. One of the purposes of the World Customs Organization's time-release studies has been to differentiate the delays caused by customs procedures from those arising from the actions of other border management agencies and from the actions of the shippers.

[4] Typical examples include government mandates to significantly increase collection of tariff revenues to meet revenue targets or the introduction of new security procedures with little thought as to their impact on trade or even the likelihood that they will achieve their stated objective.

Appendixes

Appendix A. Transactions

Table A.1. Transactions in a Typical Supply Chain

Part A	Part B		Intermediary	Documents	Payments	Information
Exporter	Importer	▷	Banks	B/L (Bill of Lading)		Order status
		◁		L/C (Letter of Credit)	L/C (Letter of Credit), CAD (Cash against documents), P.O. (Purchase Order)	Sales projection
Exporter	Shipping line	▷	Ship agent, Forwarder		Freight, THC (Terminal Handling Charge)	
		◁		Shipping order, B/L (Bill of Lading)		Estimated time of arrival, status
Exporter	Customs	▷	Customs agent	Declaration, invoice		
		◁		Customs release	VAT refund	
Exporter	Transporter	▷	Forwarder		Freight	
		◁		Consignment note		
Shipping line	Customs	▷	Ship agent	Manifest		
		◁		Permission to unload		
Consignee	Transporter	▷	Forwarder		Freight	
		◁		Consignment note		
Consignee	Customs	▷	Customs agent	COO (Certificate of Origin), pro forma invoice, packing list, declaration	Deposit, check, e-payment	Pre-arrival notice
		◁		Customs release		Duties and taxes, inspection requirement, status of clearance
Shipping line	Export gateway	▷	Ship agent	Mates receipt	Port fees, cargo-handling charges	Loading plan
		◁				Berthing availability
Shipping line	Import gateway	▷	Ship agent	Mates receipt	Port fees, cargo-handling charges	Loading plan
		◁				Berthing availability
Exporter	Export gateway	▷				Scheduled arrival
		◁		Dock receipt		
Consignee	Import gateway	▷		B/L (Bill of Lading)	Storage, special handling fees	
		◁		Delivery note		Cargo availability
International forwarder	Exporter	▷		Consolidated or house B/L (Bill of Lading)		
		◁			Freight	Cargo status

Source: Authors.

Appendix B. Potential Project Components

Table B.1. Mapping Policy Areas to Project Components and Activities

Policy areas	Project components	Improve organization and procedures	Modify policy framework	Capital investment	Assistance for institutional development	Sponsor
Tools and institutions to measure and assess logistics performance	Logistics and facilitation observatories: private sector surveys	√	√		√	PP
	Corridor performance indicators				√	G
	Port performance indicators, including dwell-time					
Institutions and regulations	Improve cross-border transport agreements		√			G
	Allow foreign trucks to transport third-country cargo in transit		√			G
	Reduce economic regulation of transport services (e.g., regulatory guillotine)		√			G
	Allow foreign participation in logistics services		√			G
Regulation of transport and logistics services	Introduce professional standards and certification for logistics service providers				√	PP
Quality, reliability of logistics services	Introduce standard performance contracts for transport and logistics services				√	PP
	Encourage development of large, long-haul trucking fleets		√	√		PP
Business practices	Create incentives to upgrade transport fleet	√	√	√		G
	Allow increased scale of logistics service providers (Mergers &Acquisitions)	√	√		√	G
	Encourage integration of logistics services for trade and distribution	√	√		√	PP
	Allow introduction of new technologies for tracking and security	√	√			G
	Introduce modern supply chain management techniques	√			√	P
	Support for a national logistics council and other mechanisms for self-regulation	√			√	G

(Table continues on next page)

Table B.1 (continued)

Policy areas	Project components	Improve organization and procedures	Modify policy framework	Capital investment	Assistance for institutional development	Sponsor
Customs modernization	Reform and automate customs procedures	√			√	G
	Improve border facilities	√		√		G
	Introduce risk management programs to expedite clearance:					
	• Reduced inspections	√				G
	• Authorized economic operators	√			√	G
	Improve trade security (e.g., scanners, secure supply chains)	√		√		G
	Integrate activities of border management agencies					G
	Introduce a single point of entry for information used in clearing cargo	√		√		G
	Promote cross-border cooperation in monitoring and clearing cargo					G
	Accept scanned copies for supporting document and e-signatures	√	√			G
	Automate and simplify procedures for sanitary and phytosanitary, and for standards certification	√				G
	Increase inland clearance of cargo	√				G
Related procedures	Simplify trade and infrastructure tariffs		√			G
	Reduce controlled commodities and certification requirements	√	√			G
Trade facilitation initiatives	Revise domestic tax policy to facilitate movement of goods within a country		√			G
	Reform banking practices related to trade, liberalize foreign exchange transactions		√		√	G
	Develop public information platforms for sharing trade and logistics data			√	√	PP
	Introduce e-government services and e-signatures to facilitate government approvals		√		√	G
	Strengthen capacity of authorities regulating trade and logistics	√			√	G
	Improve collection of key statistical information and performance indicators	√	√		√	PP
	Develop capacity to analyze indicators, monitor results of policies and investments				√	G

(Table continues on next page)

Table B.1 (continued)

Policy areas	Project components	Improve organization and procedures	Modify policy framework	Capital investment	Assistance for institutional development	Sponsor
Transit regime	Plan and manage multimodal freight corridors	√	√	√		PP
Air and sea connectivity and liberalization of services	Develop urban and line-haul transport interface (e.g., urban truck terminals)				√	PP
Public infrastructure	Increase private sector participation to provide and maintain public infrastructure	√	√		√	PP
	Introduce commercial management in port and airport operations		√			PP
	Construct new transport link			√		G
	Upgrade existing transport link			√		G
	Plan and manage multi-country freight corridor	√	√	√		G
	Establish dry ports and inland clearance facilities	√	√	√	√	G
	Develop logistics hubs (e.g., free zones, distribution centers)	√	√	√	√	PP
	Improve telecommunications services to support logistics	√		√	√	G

Source: Authors.
Note: PP=Private-Public; G=Government.

Table B.2. Mapping Policy Areas to Project Components and Private Sector Participants

Policy areas	Project components	Importer/ exporter	Clearing and forwarding	Transport operator	Terminal operator	Zone operator	Financial institutions	Information and communication technology services
Tools and institutions to measure and assess logistics performance	Logistics and facilitation observatories: private sector surveys					√		
	Corridor performance indicators					√		
	Port performance indicators, including dwell-time					√		
	Improve cross-border transport agreements	√		√				
	Allow foreign trucks to transport third-country cargo in transit	√		√				
	Reduce economic regulation of transport services (e.g., regulatory guillotine)		√	√	√			
	Allow foreign participation in logistics services	√	√	√	√			

(Table continues on next page)

Table B.2 (continued)

Policy areas	Project components	Importer/ exporter	Clearing and forwarding	Transport operator	Terminal operator	Zone operator	Financial institutions	Information and communication technology services
Regulation of transport and logistics services	Introduce professional standards and certification for logistics service providers		√	√				
Quality, reliability of logistics services	Introduce standard performance contracts for transport and logistics services	√	√	√				
Business practices	Encourage development of large, long-haul trucking fleets	√		√	√			
	Create incentives to upgrade transport fleet	√		√				
	Allow increase scale of logistics service providers (Mergers & Acquisitions)		√	√				
	Encourage integration of logistics services for trade and distribution		√	√		√		√
	Allow introduction of new technologies for tracking and security		√	√		√		√
	Introduce modern supply chain management techniques	√	√					√
	Support for a national logistics council and other mechanisms for self-regulation		√	√				

(*Table continues on next page*)

Table B.2 (continued)

Policy areas	Project components	Importer/ exporter	Clearing and forwarding	Transport operator	Terminal operator	Zone operator	Financial institutions	Information and communication technology services
Customs modernization	Reform and automate customs procedures	√	√	√	√	√		√
	Improve border facilities		√	√				
	Introduce risk management programs to expedite clearance: • Reduced inspections • Authorized economic operators	√	√		√	√		
	Improve trade security (e.g., scanners, secure supply chains)	√		√	√	√		√
	Integrate activities of border management agencies		√	√	√			√
	Introduce a single point of entry for information used in clearing cargo	√	√	√				√
	Promote cross-border cooperation in monitoring and clearing cargo		√					
	Accept scanned copies for supporting document and e-signatures	√	√				√	√
	Automate and simplify procedures for sanitary and phytosanitary, and for standards certification	√	√					√
	Increase inland clearance of cargo	√	√		√			√

(Table continues on next page)

Table B.2 (continued)

Policy areas	Project components	Importer/ exporter	Clearing and forwarding	Transport operator	Terminal operator	Zone operator	Financial institutions	Information and communication technology services
Related procedures	Simplify trade and infrastructure tariffs	√	√					
Trade facilitation initiatives	Reduce controlled commodities and certification requirements	√	√			√		
	Revise domestic tax policy to facilitate movement of goods within a country	√		√			√	
	Reform banking practices related to trade, liberalize foreign exchange transactions	√		√				
	Develop public information platforms for sharing trade and logistics data		√	√				√
	Introduce e-government services and e-signatures to facilitate government approvals							√
	Strengthen capacity of authorities regulating trade and logistics	√	√					
	Improve collection of key statistical information and performance indicators	√	√	√				√
	Develop capacity to analyze indicators, monitor results of policies and investments	√		√				

(Table continues on next page)

Table B.2 (continued)

Policy areas	Project components	Importer/ exporter	Clearing and forwarding	Transport operator	Terminal operator	Zone operator	Financial institutions	Information and communication technology services
Transit regime	Plan and manage multimodal freight corridors	√		√				
Air and sea connectivity and liberalization of services	Develop urban and line-haul transport interface (e.g., urban truck terminals)	√		√				
Public infrastructure	Increase private sector participation to provide and maintain public infrastructure			√	√			
	Introduce commercial management in port and airport operations			√	√			√
	Construct new transport link		√	√	√	√		
	Upgrade existing transport link			√	√			
	Plan and manage multi-country freight corridor	√		√				
	Establish dry ports and inland clearance facilities	√	√	√	√	√		√
	Develop logistics hubs (e.g., free zones, distribution centers)	√	√	√	√	√		√
	Improve telecommunications services to support logistics	√	√	√		√		√

Source: Authors.

Table B.3. Mapping Policy Areas to Project Components and Public Sector Participants

Policy areas	Project components	Customs	Other border	Min. of Finance	Min. of Foreign Affairs	Min. of Trade/ Commerce	Min. of Transport	Min. of Industry	Public Works	Min. of Commerce	Security
Tools and institutions to measure and assess logistics performance	Logistics and facilitation observatories: private sector surveys										
	Corridor performance indicators										
	Port performance indicators, including dwell-time										
Institutions and regulations	Improve cross-border transport agreements				√	√					
	Allow foreign trucks to transport third-country cargo in transit				√		√				
	Reduce economic regulation of transport services (e.g., regulatory guillotine)						√				
	Allow foreign participation in logistics services			√	√	√					
	Introduce professional standards and certification for logistics service providers			√		√		√			
	Introduce standard performance contracts for transport and logistics services			√		√	√				
Regulation of transport and logistics services	Encourage development of large, long-haul trucking fleets						√				
	Create incentives to upgrade transport fleet										
Quality, reliability of logistics services	Allow increase scale of logistics service providers (Mergers & Acquisitions)			√		√		√			
	Encourage integration of logistics services for trade and distribution			√		√					
Business practices	Allow introduction of new technologies for tracking and security									√	√
	Introduce modern supply chain management techniques					√					
	Support for a national logistics council and other mechanisms for self-regulation					√					

(Table continues on next page)

Table B.3 (continued)

Policy areas	Project components	Customs	Other border	Min. of Finance	Min. of Foreign Affairs	Min. of Trade/ Commerce	Min. of Transport	Min. of Industry	Public Works	Min. of Commerce	Security
	Reform and automate customs procedures	√								√	
	Improve border facilities	√	√						√		√
	Introduce risk management programs to expedite clearance: • Reduced inspections • Authorized economic operators	 √ √	 √ √								
	Improve trade security (e.g., scanners, secure supply chains)	√									√
	Integrate activities of border management agencies	√	√								√
Customs modernization	Introduce a single point of entry for information used in clearing cargo	√	√								√
	Promote cross-border cooperation in monitoring and clearing cargo	√	√		√						√
	Accept scanned copies for supporting document and e-signatures	√	√								
	Automate and simplify procedures for sanitary and phytosanitary, and for standards certification		√								
	Increase inland clearance of cargo	√	√								
	Simplify trade and infrastructure tariffs			√			√				
	Reduce controlled commodities and certification requirements			√		√					
	Revise domestic tax policy to facilitate movement of goods within a country			√							
Related procedures	Reform banking practices related to trade, liberalize foreign exchange transactions			√							
	Develop public information platforms for sharing trade and logistics data						√			√	
Trade facilitation initiatives	Introduce e-government services and e-signatures to facilitate government approvals			√		√					
	Strengthen capacity of authorities regulating trade and logistics					√		√			
	Improve collection of key statistical information and performance indicators					√					
	Develop capacity to analyze indicators, monitor results of policies and investments					√					

(Table continues on next page)

Table B.3 (continued)

Policy areas	Project components	Customs	Other border	Min. of Finance	Min. of Foreign Affairs	Min. of Trade/ Commerce	Min. of Transport	Min. of Industry	Public Works	Min. of Commerce	Security
	Simplify trade and infrastructure tariffs			√			√				
	Reduce controlled commodities and certification requirements			√		√					
	Revise domestic tax policy to facilitate movement of goods within a country			√							
Related procedures	Reform banking practices related to trade, liberalize foreign exchange transactions			√							
	Develop public information platforms for sharing trade and logistics data						√			√	
Trade facilitation initiatives	Introduce e-government services and e-signatures to facilitate government approvals			√		√					
	Strengthen capacity of authorities regulating trade and logistics					√		√			
	Improve collection of key statistical information and performance indicators					√					
	Develop capacity to analyze indicators, monitor results of policies and investments					√					
Transit regime	Plan and manage multimodal freight corridors						√		√		
Air and sea connectivity and liberalization of services	Develop urban and line-haul transport interface (e.g., urban truck terminals)										
	Increase private sector participation to provide and maintain public infrastructure			√			√				
	Introduce commercial management in port and airport operations			√			√				
	Construct new transport link						√		√		
Public infrastructure	Upgrade existing transport link						√		√		
	Plan and manage multi-country freight corridor						√		√		
	Establish dry ports and inland clearance facilities	√		√							
	Develop logistics hubs (e.g., free zones, distribution centers)					√		√			
	Improve telecommunications services to support logistics									√	

Source: Authors.

Appendix C. Report Outlines

This proposed exhaustive outline is appropriate for a TTFA phase 1 policy note. Depending on the characteristics of the assessed country or region (geography, size, and diversification of the economy), not all of the subtopics may be relevant or justified. And sufficient facts and data may not have been available for some topics to back a robust diagnosis in a phase 1 assessment.

For each of the topics and subtopics in the proposed outline (below), table C.2 links policy areas and issues with potential remedies. If the decision is made to do a more in-depth phase 2 investigation, the outline areas marked with an asterisk should be given special attention during the execution of phase 1.

The final assessment report after a phase 2 assessment should cover the same themes listed in the phase 1 outline, with sections 9 (supply chains and sector issues) and 10 (assessment of trade logistics costs) likely expanded to accommodate the focus on specific supply chains. An outline of other areas likely to be covered in a phase 2 assessment report follows the main outline; investigators may select topics from this outline depending on the scope of work and decisions made with the government to undertake specific surveys or assessments.

Outline for Phase 1 Preliminary Report

1) Trade background information

a) Main trade patterns
- principal exports and markets*
- principal imports and suppliers*
- previously identified impediments to trade and transport facilitation

b) Trade logistics patterns
- Availability of statistics
- Routes, modes, and gateway*

2) Trade logistics performance

a) Volumes*
b) Logistics performance: cost, time, reliability*
c) Arbitrage costs reliability by exporter and importers, specific commodities
d) Other issues: economies of scale, backload

3) Institutions and regulations

a) Trade policies
b) Transport policies
c) Multilateral agreements and conventions
d) Regional agreements*
e) Domestic institutions
f) Technical assistance received
g) Governance issues
h) Other border agencies
i) Trade licenses

4) Availability, quality, and performance of services

a) Logistics competence: practices and skills with consignees *
b) Trucking market structure*
c) Trucking operational performance*
d) Freight forwarding and integration*
e) Customs brokers*
f) Railways services*
g) Express
h) Banking and insurance
i) Warehousing, 3PLs (3rd party Logistics)
j) Other air cargo, river services

5) Customs facilitation

a) Customs clearance*
b) Customs regulations
c) Coordination, transparency, security, and information technology*
d) Import and export chains, main steps and structure of delays

6) Other trade facilitation

a) Trade procedures (permits and licenses for shipment)
b) Payment systems and exchange control
c) Public–private initiatives on facilitation
d) Trade promotion

7) International connectivity and transit

a) Transit systems*
b) Port and shipping connectivity*
c) Customs performance
d) Facilitation of multimodal transportation

8) Trade-supporting infrastructure

a) Roads*
b) Ports*
c) Railroad
d) Airports
e) Other backbone infrastructure

9) Supply chains and sector issues

a) Example of supply chains, assessment of logistics costs
b) Specific sector issues (e.g., special trade and customs regimes)
c) Special Economic Zones (SEZ)
d) Other issues (contracts, trade finance)

10) Assessment of trade logistics costs

a) Consolidation of available information on direct costs, overheads, and impact of inventories

b) Assessment of avoidable costs and measures with potential high gains

11) Recommendations

* Expand these sections if the decision is made to do a phase 2 assessment.

Possible added topics for a phase 2 assessment report

1) Specific supply chains and opportunities for development

a) Structure of supply chains

b) Effect of components on supply chain performance

c) Critical bottlenecks (e.g., economic regime, services)

d) Opportunities for improvement

e) Benefits

2) Domestic logistics

a) Warehousing and logistics platforms: needs and capacities

b) Distribution

3) In-depth studies

a) Skills and training needs and capacities in the private sector

b) Needs and capacity assessment of key public institutions (e.g., customs)

c) Use of information technology for clearance and tracking

d) Management of infrastructure

e) Implementation of regional agreements, notably transit regime

4) Result of surveys

a) Trucking survey

b) Exporters-importers surveys

c) Port dwell time survey

Table C.1. Policy Areas and Issues with Project Components and Remedies, per Outline Topic

Outline	Policy areas and issues	Project components and remedies
Trade background information a. Main Trade patterns 1. principal exports and markets* 2. principal imports and suppliers* 3. Previously identified impediments to trade and transport facilitation	n.a.	n.a.
Trade logistics performance a. Trade logistics patterns 1. Availability of statistics, sources 2. Volume by routes, modes, and gateway 3. Main commodities in volume b. Logistics performance: cost, time, reliability on the main routes*Arbitrage costs reliability by exporter and importers, specific commodities c. Other issues: economies of scale, backload	**Tools and institutions to measure and assess logistics performance** a. Statistical instruments for trade in volume b. Logistics performance on main routes and at gateway in terms of cost, time, and reliability	Logistics and facilitation observatories: private sector surveys Corridor performance indicators Port performance indicators, including dwell-time
Institutions and regulations a. Trade policies b. Transport policies c. Multilateral agreements and conventions d. Regional agreements* e. Domestic institutions in trade and transport facilitations f. Technical assistance received g. Governance issues h. Other border agencies i. Trade licenses	**Tariff and nontariff trade policies** a. Complexity of tariff structure for imports Nontariff barriers, such as quantitative restriction on some commodities b. Authorization regimes for imports and exports **Trade promotion and proactive policies** a. Trade promotion and market information. b. Trade finance for export **Transport and infrastructure policies** a. Comprehensiveness and consistency b. Legal landmarks **Multilateral cooperation** a. Participation in major trade facilitation agreement and fora **Regional agreements and cooperation** a. Trade b. Transportation c. Customs d. Corridor-based cooperation and institutions. e. Constraining bilateral agreements **Domestic institutions promoting trade and transport facilitation policies, mandate effectiveness and governance** a. Transportation agencies b. Customs c. Trade d. Others: trade and investment promotion, standards, health, sanitary and phytosanitary	Improve cross-border transport agreements Allow foreign trucks to transport third-country cargo in transit Reduce economic regulation of transport services (e.g., regulatory guillotine) Allow foreign participation in logistics services

(Table continues on next page)

Table C.1 (continued)

Outline	Policy areas and issues	Project components and remedies
Availability, quality, and performance of services a. Logistics competence: practices and skills with consignees* b. Trucking market structure* c. Trucking operational performance* d. Freight-forwarding and integration* e. Customs brokers* f. Railways services* g. Express h. Banking and insurance i. Warehousing, 3PLs (3rd party Logistics) j. Others: air cargo, river services	**Regulation of transport and logistics services** a. Licensing of transport—equipment and operations b. Effectiveness of freight regulations (e.g., axle load) c. Domestic and regional regulation of long-distance transport d. Procurement of imported transport equipment and spare parts e. Regulation of logistics services, including customs brokers **Quality, reliability of logistics services** a. Foreign participation in logistics services b. Availability of value-added logistics services, and conducive regulations c. Access to information on available services **Business practices** a. Shippers and consignees: market organization of demand for international and domestic logistics b. Lack of standard contracts for transport services c. Lack of standard contracts for integrated logistics services d. Integrity and business practices	Introduce professional standards and certification for logistics service providers Introduce standard performance contracts for transport and logistics services Encourage development of large, long-haul trucking fleets Create incentives to upgrade transport fleet Allow increase scale of logistics service providers (Mergers and Acquisitions) Encourage integration of logistics services for trade and distribution Allow introduction of new technologies for tracking and security Introduce modern supply chain management techniques Support a national logistics council and other mechanisms for self-regulation
Trade and customs facilitation a. Coordination, transparency, security and IT * b. Customs clearance * c. Customs regimes d. Import and export chains, main steps, and structure of delays	**Customs modernization** a. Transparency and consistency of customs clearance procedures b. Improvement of clearance and border facilities (physical and IT). c. Introduction of modern practices conducive of professionalism. (risk management, authorized operators)	Reform and automate customs procedures Improve border facilities Introduce risk management programs to expedite clearance: • Reduced inspections • -Authorized Economic Operators Improve trade security, e.g. scanners, secure supply chains Integrate activities of border management agencies Introduce a single point of entry for information used in clearing cargo Promote cross-border cooperation in monitoring and clearing cargo Accept scanned copies for supporting document and e-signatures Automate and simplify procedures for SPS and standards certification Increase inland clearance of cargo Simplify movement of cargo under bond

(Table continues on next page)

Table C.1 (continued)

Outline	Policy areas and issues	Project components and remedies
Other trade facilitation a. Trade procedures (permits and licenses)* b. Payment systems and exchange control c. Public-private Initiatives on facilitation d. Trade promotion	**Related procedures** a. Permitting of imports and exports* b. Payments methods for fees and duties c. Coordination among border agencies and procedural consistency with customs d. Implementation of single window concept, phase out of continued reliance on paper documents. e. IT readiness of non-customs procedures. f. Conflicts between trade facilitation and other public concerns (revenue, trade promotion, and market information. **Trade facilitation initiatives** a. Private participation and voice in policy making. b. Recent across the board facilitation initiatives and dedicated	Simplify trade and infrastructure tariffs Reduce controlled commodities and certification requirements Revise domestic tax policy to facilitate movement of goods within a country Reform banking practices related to trade, liberalize foreign exchange transactions Develop public information platforms for sharing trade and logistics data Introduce e-government services and e-signatures to facilitate government approvals Strengthen capacity of authorities regulating trade and logistics Improve collection of key statistical information and performance indicators Develop capacity to analyze indicators, monitor results of policies and investments
International connectivity and transit systems a. Transit systems* b. Port/shipping connectivity * c. Customs performance d. Facilitation of multimodal transportation	**Transit regime** a. Transit systems applicable on international road and rail corridors. b. Implementation of door to door regional transit systems such as TIR carnet. c. Reduction of controls at the border and en route d. Domestic and regional regulation of entry of transit operators **Air and sea connectivity and liberalization of services** a. Air transport services, passenger and cargo b. Shipping services, impact of feeder services	Plan and manage multimodal freight corridors Develop urban and line-haul transport interface, e.g. urban truck terminals
Trade supporting infrastructure a. Roads * b. Ports * c. Railroad d. Airports e. Other backbone infrastructure	**Public infrastructure** a. Road policy b. Adequacy of maintenance funding and policies c. Rail policies. d. Port development e. Improvement in service delivery (price and quality) and private participation. f. Development of logistics hubs such as logistics centers (in or not in free zones), inland clearance facilities, and dry ports/inland container depots g. Addressing congestion problems in rural areas h. IT infrastructure	Construct/ upgrade new transport link Revise maintenance policy and address gap in funding of maintenance. Introduce commercial management in port, railroad, and airport operations Increase private sector participation Plan and manage multi-country freight corridor Develop inland logistics hubs, Dry ports and Inland Clearance facilities, Encourage the development of logistics and distribution centers

(Table continues on next page)

Table C.1 (continued)

Outline	Policy areas and issues	Project components and remedies
Supply chains and sector issues a. Example of supply chains, assessment of logistics costs b. Specific sector issues (e.g. special trade and customs regimes) c. Special Economic Zones (SEZ) d. Other issues (contracts, trade finance)	**Enhancing competitiveness of key products supply chains** a. Handicap created by fragmentation of transport and logistics services. b. Efficiency of Supply chain integration for domestic distribution c. Incoterms and international contract used for the main products, dependence on foreign buyers d. Trade and customs regime to reduce production costs (drawbacks) **Synergies between facilitation and proactive trade promotion policies** a. Availability of trade finance b. Development of specific facilities and Special Economic Zones (SEZ)	
Assessment of trade logistics costs a. Consolidation of available information on direct costs, overheads, and impact of inventories b. Assessment of avoidable costs and measures with potential high gains	n.a.	
Recommendations	n.a.	

Source: Authors.

Box C.1. Policy Areas Covered in the Assessment

1. **Tools and institutions to measure and assess logistics performance**
   a) Statistical instruments for trade in volume
   b) Logistics performance on main routes and at gateway in terms of cost, time, and reliability
2. **Tariff and nontariff trade policies**
   a) Complexity of tariff structure for imports
   b) Nontariff barriers, such as quantitative restriction on some commodities
   c) Authorization regimes for imports and exports
3. **Trade promotion and proactive policies**
   a) Trade promotion and market information
   b) Trade finance for export
4. **Transport and infrastructure policies**
   a) Comprehensiveness and consistency
   b) Legal landmarks
5. **Multilateral cooperation**
   a) Participation in major trade facilitation agreement and fora
6. **Regional agreements and cooperation**
   a) Trade
   b) Transportation
   c) Customs
   d) Corridor-based cooperation and institutions
   e) Constraining bilateral agreements
7. **Domestic institutions promoting trade and transport facilitation policies, mandate effectiveness and governance**
   a) Transportation agencies
   b) Customs
   c) Trade
   d) Others: trade and investment promotions, standards
8. **Regulation of transport and logistics services**
   a) Licensing of transport—equipment and operations
   b) Effectiveness of freight regulations (e.g., axle load)
   c) Domestic and regional regulation of long-distance transport
   d) Procurement of imported transport equipment and spare parts
   e) Regulation of logistics services, including customs brokers
9. **Quality, reliability of logistics services**
   a) Foreign participation in logistics services
   b) Availability of value-added logistics services, and conducive regulations
   c) Access to information on available services
10. **Business practices**
    a) Shippers and consignees: market organization of demand for international and domestic logistics
    b) Lack of standard contracts for transport services
    c) Lack of standard contracts for integrated logistics services
    d) Integrity and business practices
11. **Customs modernization**
    a) Transparency and consistency of customs clearance procedures
    b) Improvement of clearance and border facilities (physical and information technology)
    c) Introduction of modern practices conducive of professionalism (risk management, authorized operators)

(Box continues on next page)

Box C.1 (continued)

12. Related procedures
   a) Permitting of imports and exports
   b) Payment methods for fees and duties
   c) Coordination among border agencies and procedural consistency with customs
   d) Implementation of single window concept, phase out of continued reliance on paper documents
   e) Information technology readiness of noncustoms procedures
   f) Conflicts between trade facilitation and other public concerns (revenue, trade promotion, and market information)

13. Trade facilitation initiatives
   a) Private participation and voice in policymaking
   b) Recent across-the-board facilitation initiatives and

14. Transit regime
   a) Transit systems applicable on international road and rail corridors
   b) Implementation of door-to-door regional transit systems such as TIR Carnet
   c) Reduction of controls at the border and en route
   d) Domestic and regional regulation of entry of transit operators

15. Air and sea connectivity and liberalization of services
   a) Air transport services, passenger and cargo
   b) Shipping services, impact of feeder services

16. Public infrastructure
   a) Road policy
   b) Adequacy of maintenance funding and policies
   c) Rail policies
   d) Port development
   e) Improvement in service delivery (price and quality) and private participation
   f) Development of logistics hubs, such as logistics centers (in or not in free zones), inland clearance facilities, and dry ports or inland container depots
   g) Addressing congestion problems in rural areas
   h) Information technology infrastructure

17. Enhancing competitiveness of key products' supply chains
   a) Handicap created by fragmentation of transport and logistics services
   b) Efficiency of supply chain integration for domestic distribution
   c) Incoterms and international contract used for the main products, dependence on foreign buyers
   d) Trade and customs regime to reduce production costs (drawbacks)

18. Synergies between facilitation and proactive trade promotion policies
   a) Availability of trade finance
   b) Development of specific facilities and Special Economic Zones (SEZ)

Source: Authors.

Appendix D. Mapping Policy Areas with Respondents

Table D.1. Policy Areas and Respondents Affected

Policy areas	Exporters / importers	Transport operator	Container terminal	Customs broker	Forwarder	Integrator	Warehouse	Bonded facility	Zone operator	Financial institution
Tools and institutions to measure and assess logistics performance										
Tariff and nontariff trade policies	√			√	√					
Trade promotion and proactive policies	√		√						√	
Transport and infrastructure policies										
Multilateral cooperation										
Regional agreements and cooperation										
Domestic institutions promoting trade and transport facilitation policies, mandate effectiveness and governance	√		√	√		√			√	
Regulation of transport and logistics services	√	√	√		√	√			√	
Quality, reliability of logistics services	√	√		√	√	√	√		√	
Business practices										
Customs modernization	√	√	√	√	√	√		√	√	
Related procedures	√		√	√	√	√	√	√	√	√
Trade facilitation initiatives										
Transit regime	√	√			√	√				
Air and sea connectivity and liberalization of services										
Public infrastructure		√	√		√				√	
Enhancing competitiveness of key products' supply chains	√	√	√	√	√	√	√	√	√	
Synergies between facilitation and proactive trade promotion policies	√			√					√	√

Source: Authors.

Table D.2. Policy Areas and Related Topics

Respondents / Policy areas	Type of logistics services	Supply chain	Financial transactions	Regulatory activities	Infrastructure	Level of information and communication technology
Tools and institutions to measure and assess logistics performance						
Tariff and nontariff trade policies	√			√	√	
Trade promotion and proactive policies	√		√			
Transport and infrastructure policies	√		√	√		
Multilateral cooperation	√		√	√		
Regional agreements and cooperation	√		√	√		
Domestic institutions promoting trade and transport facilitation policies, mandate effectiveness and governance	√		√	√	√	√
Regulation of transport and logistics services	√	√	√	√	√	√
Quality, reliability of logistics services	√	√		√	√	√
Business practices	√	√		√		
Customs modernization	√	√	√	√	√	√
Related procedures	√	√	√	√	√	√
Trade facilitation initiatives	√		√			
Transit regime	√	√		√	√	√
Air and sea connectivity and liberalization of services	√	√	√			
Public infrastructure	√				√	
Enhancing competitiveness of key products supply chains	√	√	√	√	√	√
Synergies between facilitation and proactive trade promotion policies	√		√	√		

Source: Authors.

Appendix E. Phase 1 Desk Research

Subjects

- **Background**
  - Geographical relationship to neighbors and major trade routes
  - Key socioeconomic data related to trade

- **Trade data**

  Possible sources: World Integrated Trade Solution (WITS), Trademap (Interational Trade Centre)
  - Commodities
  - Principal trading partners

- **Performance data (where available for individual countries)**
  - Global Enabling Trade Index, World Economic Forum
  - Competitive Industrial Performance Index, United Nations Industrial Development Organization
  - Competitiveness indicators by World Economic Forum, International Institute for Management Development (IMD), and others
  - Logistics Performance Index, World Bank
  - Business Environment and Enterprise Performance Survey (BEEPS)
  - Doing Business Survey, World Bank
  - Liner Shipping Connectivity Index, United Nations Conference on Trade and Development

- **Ports**

  Possible sources: Internet research and industry publications
  - Container traffic: inbound and outbound, loaded and empty
  - Traffic growth (Twenty-foot Equivalent Units)
  - Number of berths and ship-to-shore gantry cranes
  - Available draft
  - Yard storage area
  - Public or private operator
  - Turnaround times
  - Processing of electronic manifests and loading plans (local)

- **Road transport**

  Possible sources: International Road Transport Union (IRU), World Bank reports
  - Breakdown of road network by type and length of links
  - Road freight volume
  - National fleet by type (wheels or tonnage, fixed axle and articulated)
  - Large third-party fleet operators
  - Use of standard waybills (consignment notes)
  - Allocation of capacity (long-term contracts, urban brokers for trucking services, electronic market)

- **Rail transport**
  Possible sources: International Road Transport Union (IRU), International Road Federation(IRF), local Web site, annual reports
  - Network description including gauge, number of lands, length of network, and border crossings
  - Volume of freight traffic (bulk, loose, container or trailer)
  - Scheduled unit container trains (local)
  - Number and location of loading yards with container gantries (local)
  - Number and location of rail inland container depots

- **Shipping lines**
  Possible sources: Web sites of the major shipping lines
  - Routes served
  - Types and size of vessels
  - Scheduled services
  - Size of vessels calling
  - Proportion of direct calls and feeder calls
  - Frequency of calls
  - Schedule of services
    - Fixed interval
    - Day of week

- **Airports**
  Possible sources: Internet research and industry publications
  - Runways and length
  - Traffic volume (passengers, cargo, and aircraft movements)
  - Scheduled freighter services and belly cargo operations
  - Private sector involvement
  - Cargo storage facilities
  - Ground handling companies

- **Land borders**
  Possible sources: this information must be obtained from project reports
  - Facilities and equipment
  - Traffic (truck movements and cargo)
  - Transit times

- **Customs**
  Possible sources: World Bank's customs specialists, World Customs Organization reports
  - Single administrative documents
  - Supporting documents
  - Electronic submission
  - Clearance on documents (Green Channel)
  - Enhanced Harmonized System database (with health and agriculture warnings)
  - Inland clearance facilities
  - Transit regimes between border and inland clearance (local)

- Transit regimes between border and border (local)
- Certification of customs brokers (local)
- Revenues collected at border

- **Trade taxes**

  Possible sources: National accounts
  - Tariff bands
  - Bilateral and multilateral agreements
  - Revenues from duties and excise as portion of total tax revenues

- **Logistics service providers**

  Possible sources: Web sites
  - Designation (clearing and forwarding agents or separate agents for clearing and forwarding)
  - Freight forwarding and supply chain managers associations
  - Logistics and supply chain management curriculum
  - Industry designation for forwarders
  - Ability to issue international house bills of lading

- **Security, health, and safety**
  - Agencies responsible for inspection at the border
  - Scanning
  - Responsibility for testing imported and exported goods

- **Commerce**
  - Electronic payments for bank transactions and payments to government
  - Legislation for e-signatures
  - Business-to-business (domestic, international)
  - Typical terms of payment (invoice, CAD)
  - Access to foreign exchange accounts

- **Warehousing**
  - Large third-party operators
  - Major truck terminals and distribution centers

- **Zones**

  Possible sources: Web sites, World Bank reports
  - Location, size, occupancy, and type of firms for export processing, free trade zones, and industrial zones
  - Location and size of inland container depots and dry ports

- **Corridors**

  Possible sources: Web sites, transport sector reports
  - Defined freight corridors with development plans
  - Ministry responsible for coordinated development for multimodal corridors
  - Dedicated corridor management (if any)

- **Distribution services**
  Possible sources: Web sites
  - National overnight package services (road and air)
  - National and international retail chains
  - National distribution centers and logistics hubs

Table E.1. Research Sources

Source	Information provided by source
Airports Council International	Airfreight by airport
CIA World Factbook	Country economic data
COMTRADE, International Trade Centre (ITC)	International trade statistics: World Integrated Trade Solution (WITS), Trade Map
Containerization International	Container traffic by port
Country annual statistical report	National summary of data on various sectors, including trade and transport
DHL, Federal Express, UPS, etc.	Web sites for global forwarders
Doing Business Survey	General level of performance for trade and specific problem areas
Drewry, UK	Container freight rate
Economist Intelligence Unit (EIU) Country Reports	Trade data, macroeconomic performance, transport
International Federation of Freight Forwarders Associations (FIATA) Web site	Freight forwarders associations
International Air Transport Association (IATA)	Air freight by carrier
International Monetary Fund statistics	Macroeconomic data, Direction of Trade Statistics (DOTS)
International Road Federation	World road statistics
International Road Union	Border crossing times (TIR), transport associations
International Union of Railways	National railway statistics
Logistics Performance Index1	General level of performance for logistics and specific problem areas
Lloyd's World Shipping Directory	Shipping lines, port operators
World Port Source	Port infrastructure
UNCTAD Handbook of Statistics	Trade data
UNCTAD Review of Maritime Transport	Ports and shipping data
World Bank	Transport sector review
World Bank	Rail and road network database

Source: Authors.

[1] International Bank for Reconstruction and Development.

Table E.2. Commonly Available Data for Transport-Related Infrastructure and Facilities

Infrastructure or facility	Measures available
Airport	Number and length of runways, traffic tons loaded, discharged
Road	Length of highways, density, axle limit, gross vehicle weight limit
Truck transport	Fleet size, companies by fleet size, traffic (tons, ton-kilometers per year)
Rail	Length of lines and track, gauge, signaling, height limit, electrification
Rail transport	Fleet by wagon type, traffic (tons and ton-kilometers per year)
Ports	Depth, number of container berths and berth length, number of gantry cranes, Bulk terminal capacity, throughput (loaded TEU, tons per year)
Dry ports, inland container depots	Number and location, traffic (loaded TEU per year)
Customs	Revenues, staff, operating costs, documentary requirements, percent physical inspections, percent scanned, information technology system
Free zones, industrial zones	Location, occupancy
Freight corridors	End points, distance, modes, lanes and lines, traffic levels (average units per day)
Border crossings	Location, traffic (average trucks, tons per day)
Bonded storage	Number and location
Transit regimes	Regional or international transit regimes, licenses and carnets issued

Source: Authors.

Appendix F. Phase 1—Meetings

In phase 1 of the assessment, the investigators hold meetings with private sector associations involved in trade and logistics and with agencies that regulate these two activities. Before the day of the meeting, it is important to explain the reason for the meeting—for example, "to determine difficulties with the quality of logistics and enforcement of regulations that are a significant impediment to trade competitiveness"—and to distribute a list of topics to be covered in the meeting. It is also important to request that persons attending be familiar with these areas of concern (see below). For each type of association and government agency, the Information Guide in this toolkit provides a list of topics to be discussed at the meetings, followed by a list of questions to be covered under these topics.

At the beginning of the meeting itself, the assessor should reiterate the reason for the meeting and confirm that the opinions expressed during the meeting will not be attributed to individuals—or to the organization.

Meetings with Associations

The purpose of meeting with associations is to identify consensus about common problems and opportunities for solving these problems. When setting up the initial meetings, it is important to communicate to the association representative person organizing them that there should be a sufficient number of association members present at the meeting to provide a breadth of experience. Meetings that involve only the head of the organization or a few senior executives will generally provide information about the characteristics of the economic sector that the organization represents, but little else.

During the meeting, the list of topics sent beforehand will serve as the agenda for an open-ended discussion. The interviewer from the assessment team will be responsible for ensuring that all present participate and that an effort is made to reach agreement on the more important problems and opportunities. If no such consensus can be achieved, it is important to note the different views and suggest reasons for the divergence of opinion. Because of the effort involved in managing the discussion, at least two members of the assessment team should attend, one to guide the meeting and the other to take notes.

The time allotted for a meeting should be agreed upon in advance—one and a half to two hours when possible.

The investigators should make every attempt to ensure that those attending the meeting provide broad representation of the sector that they represent. It is also important to identify any bias the organization might have. For example, investigators should discover if the association or the members attending the meeting represent:

- only larger, better organized companies or only smaller enterprises
- companies that are foreign-owned or otherwise linked with foreign companies, or only domestic companies
- a limited set of trades or a specific region of the country, such as long-distance trucking versus local trucking
- a private-sector undertaking, or one with strong government involvement

- only certain types of activities, such as freight forwarders exclusive of air cargo.

Meetings with Government Agencies

For meetings with government agencies, the investigators should also provide a list of topics and request participation by members of the organization familiar with these topics. The purpose of these meetings, unlike those with the associations, is to identify difficulties in developing and enforcing regulations for trade and logistics services as well as for developing incentives for better logistics to stimulate the growth and diversification of trade. Therefore the participants should include senior staff familiar with each topic. The previously sent list of topics can be used as an agenda for the meeting, or the agency can determine the sequence in which the participants discuss their area of concern.

The time allotted for the meeting should depend on the number of topics and the depth to which they are to be discussed. For example, the meeting with officials from customs headquarters should include five to ten people specializing in the different regulatory activities. Because these activities and their difficulties are relatively well understood, the time required for each topic would not be extensive. In contrast, the discussions with other regulatory agencies might cover fewer topics that need more detailed discussion. A typical meeting should require one to one and a half hours. It is important that two interviewers from the assessment team attend these meetings, including one knowledgeable about the activities of the agency.

For each type of association and government agency, the Information Guide in this toolkit provides a list of topics to be discussed at the meetings, followed by a list of questions to be covered under these topics.

Appendix G. Phase 2—Selection of Supply Chains and Interview Guide Checklists

Selection of Supply Chains

Table G.1. Trade Categories—Phase 2

Origin and destination	International mode	Geographic area
Regional	Ocean	Corridor
Intracontinental	Road	Port hinterland
Pacific Rim	Air	Province
Europe/ East Coast USA	Sea–air, air–sea	Region of country
Hemisphere (East and West)		

Source: Authors.

Table G.2. Questions for Selection of a Supply Chain

- Does a significant amount of the imports and exports move by land, road, or rail?
- Are the principal markets for exports outside the region or in neighboring countries?
- If overseas, what are the major destinations?
- Are the principal imports from neighboring countries or from outside the region?
- If overseas, what are the principal sources?
- Does the country have a significant amount of trade that uses air transport?
- If so, what commodities?

Source: Authors.

Phase 2 of the assessment examines specific trades and their supply chains, defined in terms of their foreign and domestic origins/destinations and modes of international shipments (table G.1). Table G.2 provides a list of additional questions that might be used to select the trades and supply chains for phase 2 assessment.

Interview Guide Checklists

The Interview Guide in this toolkit includes checklists to be used to assist interviewers. Initially interviewers should use these checklists to structure an interview, but as the interviewers becomes familiar with the content, the checklists should be used to make sure that all of the relevant topics have been covered. An outline of each checklist is presented here, with the first level presenting the topic, and the second presenting details about the topic. The second-level details are intended to help the interviewer formulate follow-up questions if the initial response is incomplete or explain the topic in greater depth if the respondent needs more detail in order to provide an answer.

- **Type of logistics and volume of activity**
  This section covers the level of trade and volume of logistics services, providing a basis for assessing the scope and scale of the respondent's activities and for evaluating the importance of the respondent's observations. It establishes a context to weigh the importance of the recommendations presented by the assessment team later during the review.

- **Supply and value chain**
  This section examines the structure of the supply and value chain, the order cycle and processing time of individual activities, and the synchronization of supply chain components, both upstream and downstream. It includes information on the respondent's efficiency in handling goods and the quality of services offered.

- **Financial transactions**
  This section examines the transactions that occur as goods move through the supply chain—specifically, the frequency and complexity of these transactions—to identify opportunities for simplification through changes in procedures or integration of services offered by an individual logistics service provider.

- **Regulatory activities**
  This section examines the regulation of both trade and logistics services to identify bottlenecks and excessive costs due to inefficient or unnecessary regulation. Trade regulation includes restrictions on importing and exporting and the procedures for cargo clearance, both customs and health and safety. Logistics services regulation covers regulation of service providers, both economic and health and safety.

- **Infrastructure**
  This section examines problems caused by insufficient or poorly maintained infrastructure, especially transport and trade related.

- **Level of information and communication technology**
  This section examines the use of computers and electronic data exchange to expedite the transactions and improve coordination of the activities in the supply chain.

- **Problems, opportunities, and responses**
  This section allows the respondent to identify and prioritize impediments to trade facilitation. This information is used to identify consensus among the parties about the principal sources of excess costs, unnecessary delays, and poor reliability—and to solicit recommendations for mitigating or eliminating these problems.

At the conclusion, the interview should request recommendations on who else might be interviewed, using the standard list in table G.3.

Table G.3. Possible Interviewees

Importers/exporters
Exporters[1]
Importers[2]
Transport service providers
Road transport
Railways
Ocean shipping
Air freight
Container terminal operator
Logistics service providers
Customs—land border
Customs—international gateway
Clearing and forwarding agent
Integrated 3PLs (3rd party logistics)
Consolidator, storage
Bonded warehouse operator
Free zone operator
Banks
Ministries
Commerce and trade
Finance
Transport
Agriculture
Health
Export promotion agencies
Preshipment inspection

Source: Authors.

[1] Manufacturers, producers.

[2] Manufacturers, wholesalers, retailers, traders.

Appendix H. Sample Terms of Reference for Members of Assessment Team

Phase 1

Objectives

The consultant will participate in a phase 1 Trade and Transport Facilitation Assessment to be carried out according to the methodology published by the World Bank in 2010 "***Trade and Transport Facilitation Assessment***" This methodology involves meetings with stakeholders involved in specific trades. This document is also available on the GFP Web site (www.gfptt.org).

The stakeholders include associations representing importers, exporters, providers of transport and logistics services, and government agencies involved in trade and logistics. The meetings and subsequent report will cover:

- Availability and quality of logistics services and infrastructure available to exporters and importers.
- Market structure and integration with other activities.
- International competition for transport and logistics services.
- The nature of existing constraints in regulatory, documentary, and procedural requirements related to international trade transactions and corresponding transport operations.

International Logistics Expert

Responsibilities include:

- Review objectives for the assessment.
- Based on the desk research and in conjunction with the team leader select key commodities and cargoes and directions of trade that will be the subject of the assessment.
- Meet with donor organizations to discuss ongoing efforts to facilitate trade and improve logistics.
- Prepare list of associations and government agencies with whom to meet.
- Lead efforts to schedule meetings.
- Prepare agendas for these meetings and send to participants.
- Conduct meetings and prepare summary of discussions and ranking of policy areas for action.
- Conduct complementary interviews and site visits as required to confirm findings of meetings.
- Prepare a preliminary report summarizing the impediments to trade related to logistics and policy initiatives to reduce or eliminate these impediments.
- Participate in presentation of result to country director.

Based on the decision of the country director either:

- Prepare a policy note setting out the initiatives and potential benefits from changes in government policies, incentives, and investments affecting logistics services

or

- Prepare a phase 2 assessment.

If a phase 2 assessment is to be conducted, the logistics expert should:

- Work with the task manager in selecting specific trades to be evaluated.
- Prepare a sample frame including categories of enterprises to be interviewed.
- Prepare a budget for the second phase.
- Determine number of interviews to be conducted based on available funding.
- Prepare implementation schedule.
- Prepare terms of reference for assessment team.
- Assist in recruiting specialists to participate in the team.
- Revise interview checklists.
- Prepare a preliminary list of enterprises and agencies to be interviewed.

Local Logistics Expert

The local logistics expert should work with the international logistics expert in:

- Selecting key commodities and cargoes and directions of trade that will be the subject of the assessment.
- Preparing list of associations and government agencies with whom to meet.
- Preparing agendas for these meetings and sending them to participants.
- Conducting meetings.
- Preparing summary of discussions and ranking of policy areas for action.
- Conducting complementary interviews and site visits as required to confirm findings of meetings.
- Preparing report summarizing the impediments to trade related to logistics and policy initiatives to reduce or eliminate these impediments.
- Participating in presentation of result to country director.

Researcher

The researcher will prepare a desk study for the country describing its major trading activities and supporting transport and logistics services. The information collected and presented in the research report should include:

- Volume, origins, destinations, and principal international modes for major exports and imports (by commodity category—one to two digits).
- Market structure and international competition.
- Principal freight corridors for imports and exports, the transport modes on the corridors, and any information on the traffic levels.
- Volumes of freight and frequency of services at the principal gateways for international trade.
- Mapping of the major trade corridors from the production centers to the international gateway.
- Contact information for principal associations involved in international trade and transport.
- Contact information for major importers, exporters, and logistics service providers.

Phase 2

Objectives

The consultant will participate in a phase 2 Trade and Transport Facilitation Assessment to be carried out according to the methodology published by the World Bank in 2010 "***Trade and Transport Facilitation Assessment.***" This methodology involves open-ended interviews with stakeholders involved in specific trades. This document is also available on the GFP Web site (www.gfptt.org).

The stakeholders include the owners of the cargo, logistics service providers, and regulators of the trade and logistics services. The purpose of the assessment is improving trade competitiveness through improvements in logistics services, regulatory procedures, and policies related to trade facilitation. The primary tasks are to:

- Identify impediments that add to the cost, time, and uncertainty of the activities and transactions within the supply chains that serve these trades.
- Assess the relative importance of these impediments in overall supply chain performance.
- Evaluate opportunities for eliminating these impediments or reducing their impacts.
- Propose World Bank-supported initiatives to realize these opportunities.

The consultant shall conduct open-ended interviews of various agents of international trade operations to determine the structure of their supply chains, the major bottlenecks, and the effect of the quality of the logistics services on their export competitiveness. The interviews and subsequent analysis should assess:

- Availability and quality of logistics services and infrastructure available to exporters and importers.
- Market structure and integration with other activities.
- International competition for transport and logistics services.
- The magnitude of costs and delays introduced at various stages along the supply chain for imports, exports, and transit goods.
- Procedural and documentary requirements (for customs, standards, transit, transport, ports, etc.) needed to move goods from the gateways, through borders, and in transit operations.
- Information exchange and coordination between logistics service providers and government agencies.
- Complexity and effectiveness of the regulatory environment, transparency and quality of enforcement, and effect on trade competitiveness.
- Extent of competition, pricing practices, and economic regulation.

The interviews should also examine initiatives to improve trade competitiveness through:

- Regulatory and public sector reforms.
- Private sector development in the area of services (transportation, logistics, finances, etc.).

- Introduction of modern information and communication technologies related to transport and trade.
- Key investments to improve trade potential, notably along the transport corridors.
- Technical assistance measures, including training needs.

The assessment team should prepare a final assessment report that summarizes the findings from the evaluation of the interviews and recommends actionable measures. The measures should be prioritized, and a time-frame for their implementation indicated.

This assessment will focus on the following specific trades: ________. The assessment is expected to take __ weeks (see attached timeline).

Assessment Team Leader

The team leader should be responsible for managing the phase 2 assessment in accordance with the implementation plan previously prepared. Responsibilities should include coordinating:

- Arrangements for the interviews in appropriate sequence.
- Participation of the team members in the interviews.
- Team travel.
- Evaluation of the results from the interview.
- Preparation of final report.

The team leader should work together with other team members to:

- Identify additional organizations to be interviewed and assist in scheduling interviews.
- Interview representatives of enterprises and agencies.
- Prepare summaries of the information collected during the interviews.
- Compile a list of impediments affecting trade competitiveness.
- Compile costs, time, and uncertainty for components of typical supply chains.
- Assess the relative importance of the impediments to supply chain performance.
- Evaluate opportunities for reducing or eliminating the impediments.
- Develop components of a trade facilitation project to realize their opportunities.
- Prepare a final assessment report.

The final assessment report should include a summary of the observations presented during the interviews, including the impediments to trade competitiveness and opportunities for reducing these impediments. The report should also describe possible follow-up actions to achieve those opportunities that offer the greatest benefit for trade competitiveness. Where these actions will require administrative and regulatory changes, the assessment report should describe them in practical terms—including changes in organization, procedures and, if necessary, legislation to be submitted to the country government.

Assessment Team Members

The assessment team members should work under the direction of the team leader in:

- Identifying additional organizations to be interviewed and assisting in scheduling interviews.
- Interviewing enterprises and agencies.
- Preparing summaries of the information collected during the interviews.
- Compiling a list of impediments affecting trade competitiveness.
- Compiling costs, time, and uncertainty for components of typical supply chains.
- Assessing the relative importance of the impediments to supply chain performance.
- Evaluating opportunities for reducing or eliminating the impediments.
- Developing components of a trade facilitation project to realize their opportunities.
- Preparing a final assessment report.

Technical Specialist for In-Depth Studies

For the in-depth studies, terms of reference should be prepared for the specific type of problem to be addressed. These reports should have some common elements, including:

- An analysis of the problems and potential mitigation measures.
- An assessment of the expected benefits of these measures and the likelihood of successful implementation.
- Detailed proposals for implementing these measures.

Appendix I. Logistics Glossary

Air cargo agent	Independent agents or representatives of the airlines who arrange air freight shipments.
ASYCUDA	Automated System for Customs Data: a program to manage clearance developed and maintained by the United Nations Conference on Trade and Development (UNCTAD).
Automated risk assessment	Use of a computerized risk module without human intervention in the choice of risk channel.
Bonded warehouse	Warehouses in which goods can be stored that have not yet been cleared for entry into the country.
Bond	A guarantee for duties and taxes for goods entering a territory without being cleared for consumption (e.g., transit, temporary admission).
Border crossings	Extent of modernization of major crossings, including introduction of segregated lines, elevated booths to allow transactions without trucker leaving his cab, and electronic weigh scales to speed processing.
Certified customs brokers	Licensed customs clearance agents who have the exclusive right to clear cargo acting for the consignee; brokers are registered as individual meeting professional requirement.
Customs agent	A company employing certified customs brokers licensed by customs to clear cargo. It can specialize in clearance only or be an integrator of services such as a freight forwarder. The agent company may have to meet other requirement in addition to the one applying to the certified brokers it employs, for example, outstanding bonds depending on its level of business.
Electronic bank transfer	Payment of duties and taxes through a bank transfer from the consignee's bank to customs.
EDI	Electronic data interchange, an automated system to exchange trade documents. Often synonymous with electronic single window.
Electronic lodgment	Electronic submission of customs declarations by the customs officer or authorized personnel at designated locations, by a customs agent using dialup or LAN (Local Area Network), or by the consignee or customs agent using the Internet.
Factory clearance	Authorization by customs for clearance of imports at the premises of the consignee.
Freight forwarder	The freight forwarder is an integrator of services that organizes the movement of goods over one of several borders, using its own means or subcontracting one or several functions. A freight forwarding company will typically integrate the function of a customs agent and arrange transport for its client.
Guarantee for duty and tax	A guarantee for duties and taxes if not paid at the time the cargo is cleared, typically used for transit goods.
Harmonized code	The Harmonized System (HS) commodity code now used by for assigning customs duties in all countries.
ICD	Inland container depot. Usually a bonded area where loaded containers can be stored and destuffed and the cargo cleared for delivery.
Integrated database	A customs database that provides information for each commodity code on the rates for taxes and duties, a reference value, the certification requirements for the cargo, and any special handling requirements.
NVOCC	Non vessel operating common carrier. Third parties offering space on shipping lines.
Pre-lodgement	Possibility of introducing a declaration prior to the physical arrival of the goods.
Periodic declaration	Simplified clearance procedures in which the consignee does not have to file a declaration for each shipment but can, instead, file a declaration for the shipments made during a fixed period of time.
Risk assessment	The assignment of import cargo to a green, yellow, or red channel based on the perceived level of risk, with the majority going to the Green Channel, which allows for clearance without inspection upon the submission of documents.
SAD	Single administrative document. A single declaration used for imports, exports, temporary admission, and transit.
Scanners	Use of full truck X-ray scanners to inspect the contents of a truck without opening it.
Seals	Physical or eventually electronic devices used to check that a vessel (container, trailers) has not been opened. Seals are used by customs to secure goods in transit.
Shipping agent	Representative of the shipping lines who arranges for ocean shipments.

Transit	Delayed clearance system by which goods sealed and bonded can move within a territory to be cleared out of the country or to an inland destination.
T1 transit document	In the European Common Transit system, the reference transit section of the single administrative document. It is attached to a guarantee to cover the liability for the duties and taxes on cargo while transported by truck from the border to an inland clearance point. The same format is widely used in ASYCUDA.
TIR	Transports Internationaux Routiers (International Road Transport). An international transit system allowing the movement of goods in transit under a single document (carnets) and single mutually recognized guarantee for duties and taxes on cargo carried in a vehicle transiting a country. The TIR is managed by a network of national guarantors under the umbrella of the International Road Union. TIR is applicable in countries signatory of the eponymous convention supervised by UNECE (United Nations Economic Commission for Europe).
Tracing	Information system to trace whether goods, in ports or in transit, have moved beyond some milestone. It typically requires communication of information from public agencies or private operators.
Tracking	Real time tracing. Typically a purely private system for operators to locate their cargo, for example, by using the Global Positioning System (GPS).
Transport brokers	Either individuals or trucking companies that contract for both their own operations and for other truck owners.
Warehousing	Space for storage of cargo provided on a rental or lease basis. Services include to receiving, stacking, storing, unstacking, and dispatching.
Documentary credits	
Acceptance credits	Under an acceptance credit, on presentation of the stipulated documents and a draft drawn on the issuing or the nominated bank, the exporter receives a bill of exchange undertaking that payment will be effected on the designated due date.
Deferred payment credits	Under a deferred payment credit, the issuing bank and any confirming bank undertake to effect payment on a specified later date subject to presentation of the stipulated documents within the validity of the documentary credit.
Negotiation credits	Under a negotiation credit, the exporter receives an advance or an agreement to advance the funds from the negotiating bank on presentation of the stipulated documents and, where applicable, a draft.
Sight payment credits	The applicable security criteria will differ depending on the form of sight payment credit.

Appendix J. Selection Frame Components

Importers and Exporters

Specific importers and exporters are selected based on their involvement in the trades identified in the selection frame. The selection should include firms of different sizes: while larger firms have more integrated supply chains and outsource to larger logistics service providers, smaller firms have simpler supply chains and tend to use smaller logistics companies. For each trade, the sample should include both large and medium-sized companies that have a demonstrated capability for operating efficiently and growing their business.

The sample should also include local offices of multinational firms because these tend to have better organized supply chains. As small companies are usually more traditional in their operations and have little involvement in modern trade, they should not be included unless the objectives of the assessment specifically require an understanding of their difficulties.[1]

Table J.1. Sample Frame—Logistics Service Providers

Respondent category	Person to be interviewed	Classification of firms
Freight forwarder	Manager	International and domestic, large and medium-sized
Customs broker	Senior broker	Large and medium-sized
Road transport	Operations manager	Large and medium-sized
Railway	Manager, marketing or operation	By domestic region served
Shipping line	Local agent or manager	International and regional
Cargo airline	Air freight manager	International and national
Consolidator or distribution center	Facilities manager	With and without trucking services
Dry port	Facilities manager	By corridors served
Bonded storage	Manager	By location
Port terminal	Operations manager	By corridors served
Air cargo terminal	Operations manager	International, domestic
Free zone	Facilities manager	By corridors served
Banking	Export finance	Domestic and international

Source: Authors.

The number of exporters and importers interviewed must be large enough to broadly represent the designated type of trades or commodities. A reasonable target is three to four firms for each trade. Even when this number may not always be statistically representative of a particular industry, the team leader should ensure that all relevant views for that particular supply chain are included. Given limited resources to conduct the assessment, there will be a tradeoff between the number of importers and exporters and the number of logistics service providers because the former has a multiplicative effect on the latter.

The persons interviewed should be senior management familiar with efforts to expand market share and diversify into new markets, such as the managing director or marketing manager. They should be accompanied by staff members familiar with the firm's supply chains.

Logistics Service Providers

To select the logistics service providers, the assessment team's international and local logistics experts should be familiar with the multinational and domestic firms operating in the country. However, most of the sample should be selected based on referrals made during the meetings with associations in phase 1 and on the interviews with exporters and importers in phase 2. This sampling strategy assumes that the exporters and importers are involved in domestic supply chain activities: exporters do not sell ex-factory and importers do not purchase for delivery to their warehouse.[2] In this case, the referrals should provide information on the size of the firms and range of services offered. They should also indicate who in the firms to contact about supply-chain activities (see table J.1 for a typical set of logistics service providers and relevant positions within these firms).

Freight forwarders are the most important among the logistics service providers. The assessment sample should include both large and medium-sized forwarders who participate in domestic and international movements. The general manager of these enterprises is usually the most knowledgeable about forwarding activities, though in larger firms the best informant may be an assistant to the general manager. An increasing proportion of these forwarders offer a range of services, including customs clearance, cargo storage, and subcontract transport services. In this case, different persons should be interviewed to cover the questions related to their activities (for example, customs clearance, warehousing, and transport). For matters related to customs clearance, the senior customs broker in the firm should be interviewed.

For road transport, the investigators should interview both large and medium-sized companies that offer contact haulage for national—or at least interstate—shipments. In larger countries, these companies can be selected based on the corridors that they serve. Usually, the general manager is most knowledgeable about the company's operations. Very large companies are the exception, where the director of operations may be better informed about fleet operations.

For rail transport, the selection is easier because there is usually a single national provider with separate divisions or companies serving specific regions. The appropriate person to interview is the second-tier manager responsible for marketing or freight operations in the regions covered by the assessment.

Third-party consolidation and distribution services are usually provided by the larger road transport and freight forwarding companies. The managers responsible for these services can be interviewed during the visits to these companies. If there are a significant number of bonded warehouses operating outside of major gateways and intermodal yards, the manager of one of the larger facilities should be interviewed. Finally, it is important to interview one or more managers responsible for operating a distribution center or consolidation warehouse and, if possible, to include a site visit.

Site visits are also recommended for cargo handling facilities at the major international gateways. For seaports, this would involve a visit to one of the container terminals and an interview with the operations manager. For airports this would involve a visit to the cargo-handling facilities and a meeting with the manager of the cargo division. If the operations are managed by private concession, the local manager of the concession should be interviewed.

Interviews with free zone operators should be included if these facilities have been identified as an important component of import and export supply chains. Selection of a free zone should be based on its size and level of occupancy. Zones with low occupancies or older zones that do not have new tenants are unlikely to provide useful information. Interviews should be held with the general manager or marketing manager of the zone.

The final logistics service provider group to interview consists of domestic and international financial institutions providing trade finance and documentary credits. Here, the interviews should be conducted with bank executives responsible for trade finance.

Regulators

Table J.2 provides a list of regulatory agencies to be interviewed. For these, the challenge is to identify individuals at the appropriate level in the agency. Selection of both agencies and individuals should be based on referrals by contacts within the government and by the local logistics expert, as well as on referrals from exporters, importers, and logistics service providers.

Table J.2. Sample Frame—Regulators

Regulatory agency	Position to interview
Ministry of trade and commerce	Head of export promotion division
Ministry of finance	Secretary or director, duties and excise, export guarantees
Ministry of transport	Licensing
Ministry of health	Director for sanitary and phytosanitary
Ministry of agriculture	Director of quality control
Bureau of standards and testing	Director for product standards
Inland clearance facility	Officer in charge, customs
Border crossing	Officers in charge, customs and security
Border security	Regional officer in charge

Source: Authors.

For the ministries of trade and finance, the interviews should be follow-ups to meetings conducted in phase 1. The interviews should address efforts by the ministry of trade to promote trade and by the ministry of finance to tax trade flows. The persons interviewed should be senior officials responsible for these activities.

For the ministry of transport, interviews should be held with officials responsible for regulating the trucking industry. In most countries, their responsibilities would be limited to licensing and inspection of vehicles and enforcement of weight limits. For countries with more intrusive regulation, the interviews should include officials responsible for regulating contract carriers and specialized transport services such as bonded transport.

Interviews with the ministries of health and agriculture about sanitary and phytosanitary regulation and with the bureau or agency of standards about product safety should be conducted with the senior officials responsible for managing enforcement programs. These individuals are usually located at the ministry headquarters. When it is not possible to find the appropriate persons, interviews could be held with the officers responsible for these functions at the national gateways or border crossings.

For customs, there should be multiple interviews. Officials at customs headquarters should provide referrals to the appropriate facilities to visit and persons to meet. Site visits should include an inland clearance facility and a border crossing or gateway. The interviews should be conducted with the officers in charge, combined with a walking tour to permit inspection of the layout, flow of vehicles and cargo, cargo handling activities, and processing of documents. Assuming that customs is the lead agency for border management, these interviews should also cover the procedures for liaising with other border agencies. If another agency has that responsibility, a second interview should be conducted with the manager from that agency.

Notes

[1] This is not to say that smaller firms are not important for growth in trade. Rather, for the purposes of this survey, they will not provide much information on opportunities to facilitate trade because their problems are usually associated with traditional practices in organizing logistics.

[2] Exporters that sell on a CIF basis and importers that purchase on an FOB basis will have more knowledge of the international components of their supply chains. In contrast, exporters selling on FOB or importers buying CIF will only be aware of the logistics service provider that picks up or delivers the cargo to their facilities. In this situation, most of the referrals will come from the forwarders who arrange for these movements.

Appendix K. Analytical Components in Technical Studies

Technical studies should be conducted to determine the scope of a project component, its resource requirements, and benefits. These studies should apply various types of analysis:

1. **Operations analysis and management studies** to identify necessary changes in organization and procedures by logistics service providers and by the agencies that regulate their activities. An operations analysis should determine if the problem is due to physical constraints or inefficient use of available resources. It can include an evaluation of the pricing of services to determine if they provide incentives for more efficient operation. For regulatory procedures, it can identify processes that are unnecessarily complex, ineffective, or lacking transparency and subject to significant manipulation.
2. **Legal and policy reviews** to identify the formal basis for government programs and regulatory structures that prevent improvement in freight logistics and trade competitiveness. The regulatory review should identify regulations that are counterproductive, no longer relevant, or have contradictory goals. An example of contradictory goals might be encouraging competition and allowing logistics service providers to obtain a larger scale necessary to compete internationally.
3. **Design and feasibility studies** for investment in infrastructure, facilities, and equipment.
4. **Needs assessment and benchmarking studies** to design programs for strengthening government agencies, particularly those responsible for trade facilitation. Such a program might include regulation and promotion of freight logistics maintenance for transport infrastructure.

Another important component of any technical study is an assessment of the role **of public–private partnerships** in implementing the project component. For example, public–private partnerships may help achieve these project goals:

1. Improving the quality of logistics services: The private sector can provide the training, certification, and research while the government provides legal recognition of the logistics industry.
2. Introducing new technologies: The private sector is in a better position to acquire these technologies while the government must establish the preconditions for using it, such as the legal framework for electronic signatures, public investment in telecommunications infrastructure, and oversight for commercial applications of these technologies.
3. Improving public infrastructure operations: The private sector has demonstrated an ability to increase efficiency in operations and consistency in maintenance for transport infrastructure but requires the government to ensure safety and security and prevent anticompetitive practices.
4. Developing trade-related clusters: The private sector can provide commercial management to attract tenants as well as the common services needed by

smaller tenants. The government can contribute land grants, basic infrastructure, and expedited regulatory procedures to attract producers of exports and distributors of imports.

References and Bibliography

References

Arnold, John, and Theresa Villareal. 2002. "Philippines Logistics Study." Background document prepared for the Philippines Trade and Transport Facilitation Assessment, World Bank, Washington, DC.

Arvis, Jean-Francois, Monica A. Mustra, Lauri Ojala, Ben Shepherd, and Daniel Saslavski. 2010. *Connecting to Compete: Trade Logistics in the Global Economy. The Logistics Performance Index and Its Indicators*. Washington, DC: World Bank.

Arvis, Jean-Francois, Monica A. Mustra, John Panzer, Lauri Ojala, and Tapio Naula. 2007. *Connecting to Compete: Trade Logistics in the Global Economy. The Logistics Performance Index and Its Indicators*. Washington, DC: World Bank.

Raven, John. 2001. *Trade and Transport Facilitation: An Assessment Methodology*. Washington, DC: World Bank—International Express Carriers Conference (IECC).

Subramanian, Uma, and John Arnold. 2001. "Forging Subregional Links in Transportation and Logistic in South Asia." World Bank, Washington, DC.

Teravaninthorn, Supee, and Gael Raballand. 2008. "Transport Prices and Costs in Africa." World Bank, Washington, DC.

World Bank. 2004. "Syria: Integrating with Global Markets: Trade Competitiveness and Logistics Assessment." World Bank, Washington, DC.

———. 2006. "Trade Logistics and Competitiveness in Morocco." Internal document, with Morocco Ministry of Equipment and Transport. World Bank, Washington, DC.

———. 2007. "Diagnostic Trade and Integration Study: Central African Republic." Volume 1. World Bank, Washington, DC.

———. 2008. "Trade Tunisia Infrastructure and Logistics Services Development Strategy: Summary of World Bank Technical Assistance." Sustainable Development Department, World Bank, Washington, DC.

———. 2009. "Regional Cross-Border Trade Facilitation and Infrastructure Study for Mashreq Countries." Sustainable Development Department, Middle East and North Africa Region, World Bank, Washington, DC.

Bibliography

Availability, quality, and performance of services

Andriamananjara, Soamiely. 2001. "Trade and International Transport Services: An Analytical Framework." USITC Office of Economics, Working Paper 2001-11-A. United States International Trade Commission (USITC), Washington, DC.

Clark, Ximena, David Dollar, and Alejandro Micco. 2001. "Maritime Transport Costs and Port Efficiency." Policy Research Working Paper 2781. World Bank, Washington, DC.

Kumar, Shashi, and Jan Hoffmann. 2002. "Globalization: The Maritime Nexus" In *The Handbook of Maritime Economics and Business,* ed. C. Grammenos, 35–62. London: Lloyd's.

UN/CEFACT (United Nations Centre for Trade Facilitation and Electronic Business). 2007. *Guide to Trade Facilitation Benchmarking*. Geneva: United Nations Economic Commission for Europe.

UNCTAD (United Nations Conference on Trade and Development). 2004. "Assessment of a Seaport Land Interface: An Analytical Framework." Report by the UNCTAD Secretariat, United Nations Conference on Trade and Development, Geneva.

UNESCAP (United Nations Economic and Social Commission for Asia and the Pacific). 2009. *Improvement of Transport and Logistics Facilities to Expand Port Hinterlands: Policy Guidelines*. New York: UNESCAP.

World Bank. 2009. "Air Freight: A Market Study with Implications for Landlocked Countries." World Bank Transport Papers 26. Transport Sector Board and Poverty Reduction and Economic Management Network, World Bank, Washington, DC.

Customs facilitation

CEC (Council of the European Communities). 1992. *Council Regulation (EEC) No 2913/92 of 12 October 1992 establishing the Community Customs Code*. Luxembourg: CEC.

De Wulf, Luc, and Jose Sokol. 2005. *Customs Modernization Handbook*. Washington, DC: World Bank.

ICC (International Chamber of Commerce). 2004a. *ICC Customs Guidelines*. Revised. Paris: ICC.

———. 2004b. *ICC Integrity Toolkit*. Paris: ICC.

IFC (International Financial Corporation). 2006. *Reforming the Regulatory Procedures for Import and Export: Guide for Practitioners. Small and Medium Enterprise Department*. Washington, DC: World Bank.

OECD (Organisation for Economic Co-operation and Development). 2005. "The Role of Automation in Trade Facilitation." OECD Trade Policy Working Papers 22. Organisation for Economic Co-operation and Development, Paris.

WCO (World Customs Organization). 1973. International Convention on the Simplification and Harmonization of Customs Procedures. Brussels: WCO.

———. 1999. *Protocol of Amendment to the International Convention on the Simplification and Harmonization of Customs Procedures*. Brussels: WCO.

———. 2005. *Framework of Standards to Secure and Facilitate Global Trade*. Brussels: WCO.

International connectivity and transit systems

Arnold, John, G. Ollivier, and Jean-François Arvis. 2005. *Best Practices in International Corridor Management*. Washington, DC: World Bank.

UNCTAD (United Nations Conference on Trade and Development). 2003a. "Implementation of Multimodal Transport Rules: A comparative Table." UNCTAD/SDTE/TLB/2/Add. 1. UNCTAD, Geneva.

———. 2003b. "Multimodal Transport: The Feasibility of an International Legal Instrument." Report by the UNCTAD Secretariat, UNCTAD, Geneva.

———. 2003c. "The Use of Transport Documents in International Trade." Report by the UNCTAD Secretariat, UNCTAD, Geneva.

———. 2004. "Design and Implementation of Transit Transport Agreements." Proceedings from the Expert Meeting on Design and Implementation of Transit Transport Arrangements, Geneva, November 24.

UNECE (United Nations Economic Commission for Europe). 2000. "Guidelines on Public-Private Partnerships for Infrastructure: the Next Steps (PPPs)." Document presented at the Forum on Public-Private Partnerships for Infrastructure, Geneva, December 4.

———. 2007. *Customs Convention on the International Transport of Goods under Cover of TIR Carnets (TIR Convention, 1975)*. Geneva: UNECE.

WCO (World Customs Organization). 2004. *WCO Customs Compendium, Volume 3: A Secure and Efficient Transit System*. Brussels: WCO.

Institutions and regulations

Chaturvedi, Sachrin. 2007. "Trade Facilitation Measures in South Asian FTAs: An Overview of Initiatives and Policy Approaches." In *Trade Facilitation beyond the Multilateral Trade Negotiations: Regional Practices, Customs Valuation and other Emerging Issues*, 83–115. New York: United Nations Economic and Social Commission for Asia and the Pacific (UNESCAP).

De Sousa, Dariel, and Christopher Findlay. 2007. "Relationship between Liberalisation in the Logistics Sector and Trade Facilitation." In *Trade Facilitation beyond the Multilateral Trade Negotiations: Regional Practices, Customs Valuation and other Emerging Issues*, 245278. New York: UNESCAP.

Duval, Yann. 2008. "Cost and Benefits of Implementing Trade Facilitation Measures under Negotiations at the WTO: an Exploratory Survey." Working Paper 3. Asia-Pacific Research and Training Network on Trade, UNESCAP, New York.

Fasan, Olu. 2004. *Comparing EU Free Trade Agreements: Trade Facilitation*. ECDPM InBrief 6F. Maastricht, Netherlands: European Centre for Development Policy Management.

IRU (International Road Transport Union). 2004. *IRU Handbook on Road Transport Facilitation, Legislation and Practices*. Geneva: IRU.

Izam, Miguel. 2003. "Rules of Origin and Trade: Facilitation in Preferential Trade Agreements in Latin America." Serie Comercio internacional 28, Normas de origen y procedimientos para su administración en América Latina. Economic Commission for Latin America and the Caribbean (ECLAC), Santiago, Chile.

Moïsé, Evdokia. 2006, "Special and Differential Treatment in the Area of Trade Facilitation." OECD Trade Policy Working Papers 32, OECD Publishing.

Organization for Economic Co-operation and Development (OECD), Paris, France.

Raballand, Gael, Charles Kunaka, and Bo Giersing. 2008. "The Impact of Regional Liberalization and Harmonization in Road Transport Services: A Focus on Zambia and Lessons for Landlocked Countries." Policy Research Working Paper 4482. World Bank, Washington, DC.

UNCITRAL (United Nations Commission on International Trade Law).1978. *United Nations Convention on the Carriage of Goods by Sea.* Vienna: UNCITRAL.

———.1991. *United Nations Convention on the Liability of Operators of Transport Terminals in International Trade.* Vienna: UNCITRAL.

UNCTAD (United Nations Conference on Trade and Development). 2004. *Carrier Liability and Freedom of Contract under the UNCITRAL Draft Instrument on the Carriage of Goods [Wholly or Partly] [By Sea].* Geneva: UNCTAD.

———. 2005. *Capacity Building in Trade and Transport Facilitation for Land Locked and Transit Developing Countries.* Geneva: UNCTAD.

UNECE (United Nations Economic Commission for Europe). 2004. *SECI Memorandum of Understanding on the Facilitation of International Road Transport of Goods in the SECI Region.* Geneva: UNECE.

———. 2005. *UNECE Instruments to Address Trade Facilitation in the WTO Doha Work Programme: Review of Articles V, VIII and X of the GATT 1994.* Geneva: UNECE.

Wille, Patrick, and Jim Redden. 2007. "A Comparative Analysis of Trade Facilitation in Selected Regional and Bilateral Trade Agreements and Initiatives." In *Trade Facilitation beyond the Multilateral Trade Negotiations: Regional Practices, Customs Valuation and other Emerging Issues,* 27–76. New York: UNESCAP.

Supply chain and sector issues

Creskoff, Stephen, and Peter Walkenhorst. 2009, "Implications of WTO Disciplines for Special Economic Zones in Developing Countries." Policy Research Working Paper 4892. World Bank, Washington, DC.

CSIR (Council for Scientific and Industrial Research) Built Environment. 2008. *The Fifth Annual State of Logistics Survey for South Africa.* Pretoria, South Africa: CSIR.

Donner, Michel, and Cornelis Kruk. 2009. *Supply Chain Security Guide.* Washington, DC: World Bank.

FIAS (Foreign Investment Advisory Service). 2008. *Special Economic Zones: Performance, Lessons Learned, and Implications for Zone Development.* Washington, DC: World Bank.

Ojala, Lauri, and Tomi Solakivi. 2009. "International Logistic Surveys." Paper presented at the Council of Supply Chain Management Professionals' Annual Global Conference, Chicago, September 20–23.

Sarley, David, Linda Allain, and Anup Akkihal. 2009. "Estimating the Global In-Country Supply Chain Costs of Meeting the MDGs by 2015." USAID Deliver Project, Task Order 1. United States Agency for International Development, Arlington, Virginia.

World Economic Forum. 2009. *The Global Enabling Trade Report 2009.* Geneva: World Economic Forum: Geneva.

Trade and customs facilitation

Asian Development Bank. 2003. "Joint Border Processing at Regional Border-Crossings Governance." Working Paper 2. Finance and Trade Division, East and Central Asia Department. Asian Development Bank, Tunis.

GFPTT (Global Facilitation Partnership for Transportation and Trade). 2005. "Public-Private Partnerships in Trade and Transport Facilitation." GFP Explanatory Notes. World Bank, Washington, DC.

UN/CEFACT (United Nations Centre for Trade Facilitation and Electronic Business). 2005, "Recommendation and Guidelines on Establishing a Single Window." Recommendation 33. UN/CEFACT, Geneva.

UNECE (United Nations Economic Commission for Europe). 1997. "Trade Finance in Transition Economies: Practical Ways to Support Exports and Imports." Trade and Investment Guides 1. UNECE, Geneva.

———. 2000a. "Eliminating Obstacles to Efficient Trade Finance in Transition Economies: Practical Aspects." Trade and Investment Guides 5. UNECE, Geneva.

———. 2000b. "Guidelines on Public-Private Partnerships for Infrastructure: the Next Steps (PPPs)." Document presented at the Forum on Public-Private Partnerships for Infrastructure, Geneva, December 4.

World Bank. 2009. "Duty and Tax Relief and Suspension Schemes for Improving Export Competitiveness: A Reference and Learning Toolkit." Poverty Reduction and Economic Management/Trade, World Bank, Washington, DC.

Trade-supporting infrastructure

Kopicki, Ron. 2003. *MERCOSUR: A Preliminary Assessment of the Transportation Infrastructure Supporting Supply Chain Efficiency*. Washington, DC: World Bank.

Micco, Alejandro, and Tomas Serebrisky. 2004. "Infrastructure, Competition Regimes, and Air Transport Costs: Cross-Country Evidence." World Bank Policy Research Working Paper 3355. World Bank, Washington, DC.

UNESCAP (United Nations Economic and Social Commission for Asia and the Pacific). 2006. "Improvement of Transport and Logistics Facilities to Expand Port Hinterlands: Policy Guidelines" Transport and Tourism Division, UNESCAP, New York.

World Bank. 2004. *The World Bank Port Reform Toolkit*. Washington, DC: World Bank.

World Bank and Public-Private Infrastructure Advisory Facility. 2009. *Toolkit for Public Private Partnerships in Roads and Highways*. Washington, DC: World Bank.

Webography

Abbreviation	Name	URL
CSCMP	Council of Supply Chain Management Professionals	www.cscmp.org
GFPTT	Global Facilitation Partnership for Transportation and Trade	www.gfptt.org
ICC	International Chamber of Commerce	www.iccwbo.org
IRU	International Road Transport Union	www.iru.org
ITC	International Trade Centre	www.intracen.org
LPI	Logistics Performance Index	www.worldbank.org/lpi
UN/CEFACT	United Nations Centre for Trade Facilitation and Electronic Business	www.unece.org/cefact
UNCITRAL	United Nations Commission on International Trade Law	www.uncitral.org
UNCTAD	United Nations Conference on Trade and Development	www.unctad.org
UNEDIFACT	United Nations Directories for Electronic Data Interchange for Administration, Commerce and Transport	www.unece.org/trade/untdid
UNESCAP	United Nations Economic and Social Commission for Asia and the Pacific	www.unescap.org
UNECE	United Nations Economic Commission for Europe	www.unece.org
World Bank	World Bank, Trade Facilitation	www.worldbank.org/tradefacilitation www.worldbank.org/tradelogistics data.worldbank.org See RBZ Open Data Initiative
WCWCO	World Customs Organization	www.wcoomd.org
WTO	World Trade Organization	www.wto.org

Eco-Audit

Environmental Benefits Statement

The World Bank is committed to preserving Endangered Forests and natural resources. We print World Bank Working Papers and Country Studies on postconsumer recycled paper, processed chlorine free. The World Bank has formally agreed to follow the recommended standards for paper usage set by Green Press Initiative—a nonprofit program supporting publishers in using fiber that is not sourced from Endangered Forests. For more information, visit www.greenpressinitiative.org.

In 2008, the printing of these books on recycled paper saved the following:

Trees*	Solid Waste	Water	Net Greenhouse Gases	Total Energy
289	8,011	131,944	27,396	92 mil.
*40 feet in height and 6–8 inches in diameter	Pounds	Gallons	Pounds CO_2 Equivalent	BTUs

green press INITIATIVE